_Adva

As President Emeritus of Wake Tech. ———————— —————, I am proud that our institution was the first Future Forward College in an international network of innovative institutions.

At Wake Tech, faculty, staff, and students developed partnerships with other futures-oriented professionals in colleges and communities throughout the U.S. This book is one result of these successful partnerships.

Learning and Leading in an Age of Transformation provides insights and practices developed through lively, diverse collaboration, and readers will find effective approaches to expand their leadership capacities for successful futures. Master Capacity Building skills are the foundation for individuals and institutions to gain agency in an inevitable transformation process; collaboration and co-creation are some of the results. Here, the philosophy and practical applications are explained and exemplified, and the workbook provides activities applicable to any group endeavor. *Learning and Leading in an Age of Transformation* is a vital touchstone in an ever-expanding process.

Stephen Scott, Ed.D., President Emeritus, Wake Technical Community College, Raleigh, NC

****

I have been involved in Higher Education most of my career: from faculty to dean to vice president of instruction to president. Changes have occurred at an ever-increasing rate as I look back over these more than forty-five years. One of these changes is the pervasiveness of societal divisiveness in almost all areas of our lives: in education, politics, climate change, energy sources, health, etc. This book examines these changes and develops a very persuasive argument for the need for Transformational Learning for which the authors give us a clear definition.

The authors not only define transformation as it applies to learning and leadership, but they also give us detailed examples of how one can become a Transformational Leader in any organization. This is an excellent book! I wish that I had had it as the president to become more aware of the "weak signals" about the future as my group of faculty and staff leaders prepared for the future of our organization.

Larry J. Darlage, Ph.D., President Emeritus, Tarrant County College Northeast

****

Learning and Leading in an Age of Transformation is a masterpiece of creativity connecting three ideas: 1) we live in a time of historical transition between the Industrial Age and what Dr. John Cobb calls the "Ecological Civilization;" 2) education in a time of constant transformational change is very different compared to the Industrial Age when change was relatively slow; and 3) in the future, we will need to prepare citizens to connect and adapt to increasingly fast paced, interconnected, interdependent, and complex societies and economies.

Citizens will need to learn to identify emerging ideas and connect those ideas in a process of co-creation and transformation. Our ability to develop these skills will determine society's capacity to adapt quickly.

The authors of *Learning and Leading in an Age of Transformation* have taken the bold step of moving beyond incremental change of traditional ideas and methods. This ground-breaking book asks the reader to rethink how systems of leadership and learning will need to be redesigned for societies and economies in which all aspects are transforming. The authors provide specific guidance for leaders who will need to be prepared to support these efforts. We need more pathfinders like these.

Rick Smyre, CEO, Communities of the Future, and co-author of *Preparing for a World that Doesn't Exist – Yet: Framing a Second Enlightenment to Create Communities of the Future*

****

Something has gone wrong. Ours is not the world we were promised. Even absent COVID, the early decades of the 21st Century, for far too many of us, have been traumatizing, disorienting and exhausting.

It is within this perspective that I, as an internationally recognized pioneer in Canada of serious futures research, applaud the authors of *Learning and Leading in an Age of Transformation* for their insight, caring and creativity.

They have created a volume that will be especially useful to persons who are beginning to take seriously that the deepest aspiration of our Modern Techno-Industrial (MTI) cultures is wrong and wrong-headed, namely the desire to improve our modern world and extend it virtually forever in both time and space.

This volume is a fine introduction to the new work of the 21st Century – learning to transcend the presuppositions, aspirations and criteria for success of our now almost fully modern MTI world. This book will get you onto a road less travelled; a road we all need to be on.

Ruben F. W. Nelson, Executive Director, Foresight Canada

Learning and Leading in an Age of Transformation

A book in the living in an age of transformation series

M. Jayne Fleener, Magdalena H. de la Teja, Benita Budd, Emily Moore, and John C. Carver

ISBN 978-1-64504-275-4 (Paperback)

ISBN 978-1-64504-276-1 (Hardback)

ISBN 978-1-64504-277-8 (E-Book)

Library of Congress Control Number: 2022943739

Printed on acid-free paper

This book is Volume 1 of *Living in an Age of Transformation*

Series Editors: M. Jayne Fleener, Rick Smyre, and Magdalena H. de la Teja

Dedication

We dedicate this book to all of our past and future students and colleagues for their continued work to transform the future. We also dedicate this book to our families whose support has been instrumental in completing this project and supporting us to carry on this work. And finally, we dedicate this book to Rick Smyre and his spouse, Brownie (in memoriam). Rick's generosity of intellect, inspiration and time has nurtured this project from the conception and without whom Communities of the Future would not exist.

Table of Contents

List of Figures & Tables   xiii

Foreword   1

Preface   3

Chapter 1   7
Transformational Thinking
Introduction   7
    Coming into Focus   7
    Going Forward   8
    How Do We Get There from Here?   9
Transformational Thinking   10
    Life is Growth and Change   10
    New Ideas and Transformational Changes   11
    Understanding the Difference Between   13
      Reforming and Transformational Change
    Developing Capacities for Learning   14
    Learning, Unlearning and Uplearning   15
Transforming Public Education   18
    Transformational Change is Not a Straight 18
      Line
    Making Connections Among New Ideas   19
    Building Parallel Processes   24
    Learning Ecosystem Design Essentials   25
    Learning in the Age of COVID   26

Teaching and Learning at 60,000 Feet   28
Teaching and Learning at 10,000 Feet   28
Summary   29

Chapter 2   31
Futures Generative Dialogue
Strategies for Futures Generative Dialogue   32
    Finding Consensus and Getting Centered   32
    Rethinking Fundamental Freedoms   33
    Asking the Right Questions   35
    Facilitating Interlocking Networks   35
Global Communities   36
    New Normal   36
    Technological Innovation   37
Through the Looking Glass   37
    Personal Reflection   37
    Reform, Transform, or Both?   38
Teaching, Learning, School & Society   41
The Countdown and the Launch   43

Chapter 3   45
Learning in Transition
Introduction   45
    Personal Reflection   45
    Standing at the Precipice   46
The Third Rail   48
    Personal Reflection   48
    Seeds of Doubt   50
Learning Myths   51
    Social/Economic Learning Myths   52
    Educational Myths   55
Pervasive Learning   59

Chapter 4   67
Building Relationships with the Future
  A New Relationship with the Future   69
    Linear Time   69
    The Expanded Now   70
    Developing a Relationship with the   73
      Future
  Adaptive Futures Learning   75
    Personal Reflection of Unexamined   76
      Assumptions
      Weak Signals   78
      Missed Opportunity   78
  Futuring Techniques   79
      Futures Wheel   79
      Futures Triangle   83
      Integral Futures Matrix   84
      Causal Layered Analysis (CLA) 88

Chapter 5   93
Creating Futures Learning Ecosystems
  Flexible Learning Spaces   94
    Personal Reflection   95
    Educational Contours   96
  Lifelong Learning   98
  Futures Literacy   101
  Connective Individualism   102
  Ecosystem Engagement   103

Chapter 6   107
Framework for Transformational Leadership
  Foundations for Master Capacity Building   108
    Transformational Leadership   108
      Development
    Master Capacity Building for Transformation 109

Related Theories and Writings 112
   Connectivism 112
   Theory U 113
   Growth Mindset Nurturing Mindflex 115
Transformational Leadership Principles 115
   Employing Adaptive Planning for Complex Adaptive Systems 118
   Collaboration Station Example of Futures Generative Dialogue 119
   Asking Appropriate Questions 120
   Engaging Connective Listening 120
   Designing and Using Ecosystems 121
   Designing & Utilizing Parallel Processes 122
   Identifying Access Points and Interdependence 124
   Supporting Self-Organizing Groups and Deep Collaboration 124
   Example – Self-Organization and PAUSE 125
   Sustaining Self-Organizing Transformative Ecosystems and Cells 126
   Creating Transformative Cells 126
   Gamestop Example of Transformative & Interactive Cells 127
   Higher Education Example of Transformative Cells 127
   Supporting Transdisciplinary Thinking and Interaction 128
   Example of Adaptive Planning to Support Transdisciplinary Thinking 128
Supporting Transformational Learning 128
Identifying Weak Signals and Emerging Trends 129
Weak Signals and the Coronavirus 129
Summary 130

Chapter 7   133
Interconnecting Actions & Activities
  MCB Strategies to Leading Transformation   134
    Adaptive Planning for Complex Adaptive   134
      Systems
    Asking Appropriate Questions   135
    Connective Listening/Creative Connections   136
    Creative Connections: And/Both (versus   137
      Either-Or)
    Creative Connections/Linear and Non-   137
      Linear Capacity Building
    Identifying Access Points and Interdependence   138
    Moving In and Out   139
    Parallel Processes   140
    Reflecting and Connecting   141
    Seeding New Ideas   142
    Unlearning and Uplearning   142
  Conclusions   144

Chapter 8   145
Engaging Strategies for Transformation
    Transforming the Teaching/Learning   146
      Paradigm
    Transforming the Community Development   147
      Paradigm
    Transforming the Economic Paradigm   148
    Transforming the Workforce   148
    Transforming Workforce Development   149
    Transforming by Reimagining Infrastructure   150
    Transforming Education (All Levels)   151
  Forward Looking Thoughts (Disruption and   153
    Regeneration)
  Conclusions   154
    Navigating the Ecosystem of Learning   155

for the Second Enlightenment

Ponderings for Learning in an Age of   156
    Transformation

Developing Transformational Leadership   157
    Capacities

Future Forward Learning   159

References   161

Acknowledgements   165

Appendices   167

Index   189

About the Authors   197

About Communities of the Future   201

List of Figures and Tables

Figure 1.1: Smyre & Richardson (2016) Essential Skills for Engaging Transformation.   10

Figure 1.2: Educational Conformity Visualized   12

Figure 1.3 X-1 Plane   17

Figure 1.4 Evolution of Humankind   18

Figure 1.5 Learning Ecosystem Parallel Processes   24

Figure 2.1 Merry-Go-Round Experiences   32

Figure 2.2 What Kind of Work Do You Do?   43

Figure 3.1 Social and Educational Myths   59

Figure 3.2 Lessons from Informal Learning   63

Figure 3.3 Learning Terrains – Content Maps Versus Curriculum Contours   65

Figure 4.1 Dewey's Event Epistemology and Memories of the Past   71

Figure 4.2 Expanded Now Experiences   72

Figure 4.3 Adaptive Futures Cone   75

Figure 4.4 Futures Wheel for COVID-19   82

Figure 4.5 Futures Triangle   83

Figure 4.6 Integral Futures Matrix   84

Figure 4.7 Example of IF Approach to Overcoming   88
    Myths & Addressing Transformational Challenges

Figure 4.8 Causal Layered Analysis   89

Figure 4.9 CLA Example – Food Insecurity   91

Figure 5.1 Futures Learning Ecosystem   94

Figure 6.1 Seven Moments of Theory U and the   114
    Expanded Now

Figure 6.2 Master Capacity Builder's Toolkit   130

Figure 7.1 Master Capacity Builder Strategies   144

Table 1.1 First Order and Second Order Change   13

Table 1.2 Learning in the Age of COVID example   26

Table 6.1 Traditional Versus Transformational   117
    Leadership

Foreword

Rick Smyre

In 1989, a group of twelve people from North and South Carolina met at Wilmington, NC to ask the question, "how do we get people in the Southeast interested in thinking about the future." From the dialogue of that weekend was birthed the idea of Communities of the Future (COTF). Over the next thirty years, a network of people in forty-seven states in the U.S. and eleven other countries of the world has evolved, working in collaboration to develop new concepts, methods and techniques of community transformation. A virtual COTF Center was established in 1993 using the Internet to network those involved. The COTF Network continually "morphs" by adding "nodes" through collaboration with existing people and organizations throughout the country when new COTF concepts and methods are created.

Based on the idea that we are living in a time of historical transformation, the Communities of the Future Network has focused on a new concept of leadership called Master Capacity Builders to develop new "capacities for transformation" capable of helping local areas prepare for a constantly changing, interconnected and increasingly complex society. Over the last decade, it has become apparent that many principles, concepts and methods of an Industrial Age society have become increasingly obsolete. Communities of the Future is an experiment in community research and development to identify and develop new approaches to how we do economic development, how we govern, how we educate/learn, how we create a community-based system of preventive healthcare, how we lead, and especially how we think.

This book is the first in what is anticipated to be a series of books about how Communities of the Future approach ideas and principles to disrupt, create, and transform all sectors of society including education, the economy, healthcare, business, technology and democracy. The focus of this volume is on transformational needs and strategies for rethinking education and leadership at all levels. Beginning with a focus on the current challenges to education and explorations of emerging metaphors and perspectives for the future of education, this book provides useful guidance and explicit activities for creating transformative leaders and learners. With an emphasis on futures learning needs and strategies, master capacity building skills are explored that support new ways of thinking and doing necessary during these times of rapid change.

This book ends with a series of activities designed to facilitate the implementation of master capacity building principles with a variety of groups of individuals. Working towards community and social transformation, these activities support the theoretical and discursive focus of the book on leading and learning futures.

The authors of this book bring a wealth of practical and scholarly backgrounds to inform their thinking and facilitate their ability to communicate to a wide range of audiences. Their differing perspectives and experiences converge to offer the reader a rich array of ideas and understandings of how to create communities of the future.

Preface

Learning has always been foundational to the growth and survival of societies and civilizations. The socio-economic system of learning that emerged at the turn of the 20th century and was cultivated for the last 100 years was linear, grounded in consumerism, instantaneous gratification, one best answer, standardization, and competition. We are now living in a time of radical change, similar to the kinds of societal transformations occurring during the Renaissance period in the 13th and 14th centuries. As Kuhn (1957) described in *The Copernican Revolution* and later reinforced in his *Structure of Scientific Revolutions* (1962), these kinds of societal transformations are rare. But after over 500 years, when the Renaissance brought in the Modern Era, it seems we are on the precipice of significant social, economic, environmental, technological, political and artistic (STEEPA) change. But this time of rapid change brings with it dire consequences to the actions and directions we choose. We are at a turning point where we have an opportunity to set new directions to transform society, or to maintain on our current destructive path that will ultimately exacerbate the crises we are now facing across all STEEPA categories of human endeavor and potentially destroy civilization and democracy as we know them.

This book provides visions for transformational learning ecosystems for the future, including a different perspective of the kind of transformational leadership needed for these shifts. The emergent civilization will need new ways of thinking and interacting to overcome existing challenges of divisiveness, desires to return to past ways of thinking and doing, and maladaptive myths about success and progress that pit individuals and groups against one another. The modern vision of success and its underlying expectations for unending advancement and growth are unsustainable and are in need of transformation. Communities will need to develop new ways of interacting and thinking that will require new ways of learning and knowing, supporting the need for transformative capacities and leadership for emergent times and unknown futures.

This book is designed for everyone who cares about the future. While the initial focus is on education, the ultimate goals of this book are to support new ways of thinking, learning and being and provide guidance for a new kind of leadership that applies to all individuals as they navigate the unknown demands and address the current challenges facing our divided and uncertain society. At stake is our very forms of life, democracy, freedom, environmental and civilizational sustainability.

Beginning with an exploration of learning ecosystems and futures generative dialogue in Chapters 1 and 2, the role of learning is discussed and potential pathways for transforming public education are presented. Underlying the need to change formal education is the need to rethink the kind of learning and knowing that is important for the future. Questions about how we can educate the next generation of children to be futures literate point to the need for new capacities for making connections, consensus building, asking the right questions, and participating in interlocking systems of meaning and purpose.

Chapter 3 extends these learning needs for the future and shows how current ideas about what it means to know and learn are maladaptive for the rapid and transformational changes occurring across all STEEPA dimensions of society. Social, economic and educational myths about how we prepare to live successfully in a modern society are challenged as new myths and metaphors are posited. The need for ubiquitous, pervasive, "learning at the speed of need" will require an emphasis on learning as something that happens in informal as well as formal settings to developing learning approaches that will carry one throughout a lifetime. Rather than a roadmap to learning as explored in a standard curriculum, a new learning terrain is needed to help individuals and groups navigate through transitional and transformative changes throughout their lifetime. These new learning demands require new capacities for transformation, collaboration, and connection. Specific futures learning techniques are explored to provide models for readers to begin to develop futures learning skills.

Chapter 5 extends on these notions of futures learning skills, capacities and dispositions to discuss how to develop flexible learning spaces within formal educational settings and informal, community settings within a society. Lifelong learning, futures literacy and connective individualism become important for the kind of ecosystem engagements necessary to transform our society to meet the many challenges we face today.

Chapter 6 introduces the notion of master capacity building leadership as important to the nurturing and support of futures learning at all levels of society. The discussion of master capacity building (MCB) leaders is important for formal as well as informal leaders to understand the different kinds of skills and dispositions needed for adaptive planning and interconnected living during times of rapid change. Foundational theories for MCB leadership are presented, supporting transformational change and democratic participation for creating communities of the future.

Chapters 7 and 8 explore the 12 strategies for MCB leaders by providing specific action guides and discussions of how to work with communities and collectives of individuals towards transformative change. Building on to the ideas of futures learning perspectives, the MCB supports futures learning across different contexts to prepare and provide for full participation during transformational engagements. Developing transformational leaders will be extremely important for navigating future learning ecosystems and developing the kinds of futures learning skills and dispositions required to promote and advance radical change. The appendices provide specific samples for MCB leaders to use with groups of individuals.

The theoretical and practical approaches of each chapter of this book address important understandings and explorations of possible, plausible and desirable learning futures during transitional times, important for educators and non-educators to understand with direct implications for global, national, and local business, industry and communities of the future. As pervasive learning and ubiquitous technology become more dominant, what it means to be educated and a contributing member of our global society will change.

Our expectation is that this book will benefit a diversity of people across religious and political affiliations, racial identities, and geographical locations in the world. We hope readers will gain a better understanding of the urgency of learning how to be adaptable and be transformational in preparing for changes that are increasingly interconnected, interdependent, constant and complex. The book encourages us to remain mindful and inspired that we have the capacity to learn to be collaborative and humanistic in confronting the big global issues (e.g., climate change, poverty, migration, renewable energy sources, health and well-being, peace, etc.) of our world now and into the future.

Chapter 1

Transformational Thinking

Introduction

Coming into Focus

As mankind transitions from the 20th to the 21st century, great discourse is happening. With the rate of change accelerating exponentially and life expectancy lengthening to 80+ years old, coupled with years of shifting and sorting by chronological age, the interaction of these trends has caused different generational perspectives and beliefs to come into conflict. Deep beliefs about religion, sexuality, society, social structure, marriage, and family as well as the definition of community and success, are all being challenged. In the United States as well as many countries across the globe, the struggle for power and control between old vs new, legacy and traditional vs. transformational and evolutionary are being played out politically. We have entered a period of evolutionary and transformational change.

Much has been written and said on the need for the transformation of our teaching and learning, educational systems. A wide range of educational elements have been identified and reflected upon as requiring transformation, including structure and organization, what is taught and how it is taught, use of time, classroom organization and appearance, and how these are all funded, as well as, at its most basic level, what is most important to learn. Foundational norms from the last 100 years are being stressed and questioned as to their validity and relevance. It is important to realize the present educational system of teaching and learning is but one of many current institutions now in a period of historical transition.

The protocols, structures, actions, and systems that have been applied to teaching and learning were done with the best of intentions. What was known and believed to be true at the time, along with the application of the perceived body of knowledge and understanding, was integrated into teaching practices and assessments. Because this was strategic and deliberate, subliminally the educational goal in the United States was to build conformity and consumers, not innovators or creators. The belief that the public education was the melting pot and equalizer of the American experience is being challenged today by the perception that schools have reinforced social class division and there exists unequal educational opportunity based on a person's zip code.

Going forward

Just as the caterpillar builds a cocoon from which a butterfly emerges, mankind has built a cocoon of 20th century beliefs and experiences, and now is beginning the process of emerging as a 21st century butterfly. This transformation is something not to fear but to be embraced. The advantage mankind has over the butterfly is the ability to learn from and build on past experiences.

To this point, the intent has been to look back, identifying patterns and conditions to realize that we are going through a normal process of evolutionary growth. Every cycle of transformation has a beginning, middle and end, and each of these "cycles of life" overlap each other. The amount of time for transformation and transition varies. There is not a clean break from the end of one cycle to the beginning of the next. In the future, transformation will mean that the past will not give us a path to the future, because the accelerating future will be very different from the past.

That being said, to begin to envision a new system of learning, the "purpose" question must be understood. What was the purpose of schools and the formal education process? Is that purpose still valid today?

How do we get from here to there?

The current volume of content being created around change is huge. Daily it seems that authors, bloggers, and influencers are digitally putting out perspectives, opinions, and research for consumption. Contemporary book titles like Brene Brown's (2015) *Daring Greatly*, to *The Innovator's Mindset* by George Couros (2015), *Too Fast to Think* by Chris Lewis (2016), *Answering Why* by Mark Perna, and Dennis Shirley and Andy Hargreaves's (2012) *The Global Fourth Way* paint a picture of change and transformation. TED talks, Twitter chats, Instagram and Facebook speak to a type of transformational change in which new thinking is needed, as well as focusing on the importance of developing human capital in new ways. Crucial is the courage and strength to let go of the past and seek the quickly emergent new.

Rick Smyre and Neil Richardson in their book (2016), *Preparing for a World That Doesn't Exist – Yet*, have developed thinking and skill sets to facilitate systemic transformational change. Identifying eleven conditions for consideration, Smyre and Richardson set out a roadmap for understanding the why as well as building the skill sets to get to the New World (see Figure 1).

The intent of this chapter is to link personal observations and experiences of navigating through change through the lens of Smyre and Richardson's work. A key goal will be connecting with others to create a synchronicity of thought, effort, energy, and action for transformative change. The goal is to come together to co-create focus and structure for learning and teaching in the 21st century.

Figure 1.1: Smyre & Richardson (2016) Essential Skills for Engaging Transformation.

11 Essential Skills for Engaging Transformation

- Understanding the Difference Between Reforming and Transformational Change
- Listening for Value
- Concepts of Risk Taking
- Asking Appropriate Questions
- Connective Thinking
- Building Parallel Processes
- Futures Generative Dialogue

- Looking for Access Points and Laying Seeds
- Use of the Principles of Complex Adaptive Systems
- Introducing Weak Signals and Future Trends & Their Impact
- Design and Facilitation of Interlocking Networks

Smyre & Richardson, 2016

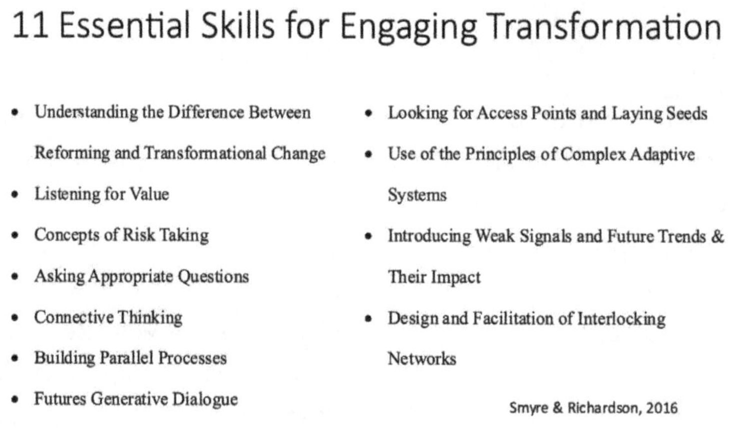

Transformational Thinking

Life is Growth and Change

It seems the evolution of mankind historically follows similar storylines, only to be revised and updated with each generation's experiences, discoveries and understanding. If one accepts that within the history of mankind there exists repetitive patterns, then studying the success, achievement and failures of these patterns will empower mankind to make good choices as humanity evolves. In times of historical transformation there is a need to rethink totally what has worked in the past.

The First Enlightenment followed the Middle Ages as a result of increased interactions between different cultures, re-discovering ancient texts, a new system of thought called humanism[1], technology innovations and the impact of conflict among competing ideas. The Black Plague pandemic disrupted that time, just as COVID-19 has disrupted current time. All this sounds familiar from today's perspective.

The term Renaissance Man or Woman is used today to describe a very clever person who is good at many different things. In reference to the First Enlightenment, they were the visionary early adopters, comfortable with change and new thinking. These characteristics and depositions are desirable outcomes in the creation of a Second Enlightenment Learning Ecosystem.

New ideas and transformational change. Linking to the past.

Learning has always been foundational to the growth and survival of societies and civilizations. Each has applied its beliefs and perspectives on organizational structure to learning and the role of educating youth. The socio-economic system of learning that emerged at the turn of the 20th century and cultivated for the last 100 years was linear, grounded in consumerism, instantaneous gratification, one best answer, standardization, and competition. Oneself, personal accomplishments and accumulation of wealth were priority and determined social status.

The 20th century industrial system-thinking components of mass production, interchangeable parts, and time on task were applied to design a process to teach already defined knowledge, thinking and reason. The system conditioned and prepared the learner to fit societal needs and embrace norms and beliefs that

---

1   Humanist beliefs stress the potential value and goodness of human beings, emphasize common human needs, and seek solely rational ways of solving human problems.

had developed over time and focused on making traditional thinking and old ideas more efficient. Indoctrination was just as mission critical as memorization of knowledge. Conformity and standardization were prioritized over creativity and imagination.

Figure 1.2: Educational Conformity Visualized

Societal stereotypes, bias and norms were reinforced intentionally and unintentionally, specifically, or subliminally, throughout the educational system. Consumerism, fueled by instant gratification, reinforced by mass media campaigns, as well as cultivating feelings of risk avoidance, worked to condition the population to think in terms of classical ideas and learning.

Over time, generations of individuals have been stimulated and programmed to embrace these thoughts and conditions. *The degree/success to which a person accepted or rejected these beliefs caused a societal "zoonosis syndrome" with potential to harm one's mental and or physical well-being significantly.* (Depression, Anxiety, Alcoholism…all symptoms of not being able to "fit into" society norm or lack of success as defined by that norm.)

As we transition from the 20th century Industrial Age to the yet to be named 21st century age, systems, thinking, and beliefs are being challenged, evolving, and transforming. Looking back at what was once normal is now giving way to new normal and transformed realities. Compounding the complexity is that four generations of adults are alive, each with perceptions and mental models of what is "normal" shaped by historical and current experiences, trying to figure out what is next. Because of the COVID-19 pandemic, all are having to be reframed at the same time. Because of technology, change is accelerating exponentially and "transforming" all aspects of society. Thus, the name "transformational" thinking.

Understanding the Difference Between Reforming and Transformational Change

Change is constant, complex, and could be classified as either 1st-order (reforming) or 2nd-order (transformational).

Table 1.1 First-Order and Second-Order Change

First Order Change	Second Order Change
An extension of the past	A break from the past
Within existing paradigms	Outside of existing paradigms
Consistent with prevailing norms, values	Conflict with prevailing norms, value:
Incremental	Complex
Implemented with existing knowledge and skills	Requires new knowledge & skills
Implemented by experts	Implemented by stakeholders

Walters, EdD, T. (2004). The leadership we need: using research to strengthen the use of standards for administrative preparation and programs. *Mid-continent Research for Educating and Learning.*

Both first- and second-order changes can lead to transformational change although neither type of change guarantees predictable or sustained transformational change. In both instances, facilitating transformational change takes energy and courage. The change needed to get to the world "that doesn't exist – yet" means embracing new knowledge, looking at the context in which knowledge and beliefs exists, and being ready to move to create new mental models.

Developing Capacities for Learning

Webster's Dictionary defines learning as *"to gain knowledge or understanding of or skill in by study, instruction, or experience."* Historically, knowledge and understanding of a new skill, and the means to deliver and assimilate it, were based on what was believed to be true *at the time.* The existing educational system was designed to be linear and one dimensional with a focus on content of knowledge, and an understanding of a skill application in one discipline, in isolation. Little, if any, consideration was given to application of knowledge, understanding or skill across connected disciplines in real world situations that were either predictable or unpredictable. There was the belief that there was one correct answer, derived by one sequence of events, that could be replicated by mass standardized instruction and assessment.

Accomplishing this meant sorting kids by chronological age and not by emotional, social and intellectual readiness. Learning was limited by time and the expertise of the assigned classroom teacher, with content presented in isolation with no context or connections. Assessment and academic growth were measured on standardized tests with grading based on percentage of answers correct, often resulting from the memorization of facts.

Today, school closures due to COVID-19 have added to design flaws in the current system of learning. *Conditions and context have radically changed, and schools (and families) are struggling to adapt.* In post-COVID-19 public conversations, the phrase "catching students up academically" creates the question "catch them up to what?" It illustrates the historical mental model that at a certain age, at a certain time, students should know a prescribed amount of knowledge.

This comment opens a door for transformational leaders to introduce the concept of "Transformational Learning." The idea of "catching up" can be considered within a traditional scope and sequence or redefined by what it means to "catch up" when the overall society and economy is transforming. The first approach focuses on efficiency of learning principles and methods that already exist. A transformational approach looks to find connections among totally disparate ideas as a way to prepare for a world that is very different from the past. As a result, ideas such as "connectivism" (Seimens, 2004, 2005) become key to the ability of our education system to be able to adapt to a new type of constant change whose undergirding principles are truly transformational. This is at the basis of the need to rethink totally how we educate our population in ways that allow them to develop "capacities for transformation."

Learning, Unlearning and Uplearning: Listening for Value

New academic "connection points" and mile markers need to be established based on mastery and proficiency. In parallel, there is the need to build new capacities in the thinking of students so that they can see creative connections among emerging ideas that have not existed in the past. This means really looking hard and creatively for connections among disparate ideas as well as providing operational, personalized, differentiated instruction. Individualized education plans for all students are on the horizon to help all students learn to adapt to constant, transformational change.

It was once believed that the world was flat, and that bloodletting would cure illnesses. Could it be that, in the future, current instructional practices of today will be looked on as being as crazy as medieval beliefs and medical practices?

Unlearning becomes a new kind of learning skill that involves the risk of challenging old ways of thinking, doing or being. It involves risk taking to not be wed to tradition and the comfortable. Unlearning is important for transformational thinking and is a mindset or skill that is wedded to transformative thinking. Value shifts away from tradition to context, meaning, and emergence. In this way, unlearning requires embracing risk.

Mankind is experiencing a new kind of discourse centered around risk. There is an extreme fear of what may be next, and with that, a redistribution of power. There is a fear that a redistribution of power could bring governments and forms of governments like democracy to their knees due to the fact that there is a great segment of our global society who are scared that the future will leave them behind. As a result, many citizens desire to revert back, or at least, stay the same in ways that they still understand.

Going back to traditional ideas and methods is as impossible as stopping the rotation of the Earth. For many, the uneasiness and uncomfortable feelings of transformational change can be equated to the stages of mourning: *shock and denial, anger and depression, acceptance and hope.*

Preparing for a different kind of society and world that will ensure hope means letting go of power and traditional mental models, systems, relationships and structure so as to discover and embrace new thinking and realities. For many who are comfortable with 20th century approaches and have benefited from them, and who avoid risk, this kind of unlearning risk is quite unnerving.

When Major Chuck Yeager first broke the sound barrier in the rocket plane X-1, he had to accelerate from "normal" through extreme turbulence. To break the sound barrier required the technology, and energy of the X-1 rocket plane as well as the strength and courage of pilot Chuck Yeager. Major Yeager reported moving through great turbulence before the X-1 traveled straight and smooth on the other side of the sound barrier. This is analogous to experiences of the shock of historical, transformational change.

Figure 1.3 X-1 Plane

We are now in the turbulence of historical change and have yet to break through to the other side. The quicker we can let go, move through the turbulence of shock, denial, anger and depression to acceptance and embrace the new, the quicker we will flourish, grow, create, and achieve. We must find the courage to move through the turbulence and get to the smooth emergence on the other side. Like the earth's continued rotation, transformational change cannot be stopped.

A crucial step forward is to engage in meaningful collaboration and discussion of diverse perspectives with the attempt to identify and understand a new type of society that is only recently (in historical terms) beginning to emerge. This involves uplearning. It is important for us to learn how to move though disagreements, find common ground and build consensus on emerging possibilities. This will be more than a challenge to the foundations of current mental models: beliefs, family, faith and being. It will require true transformation.

Transforming Public Education? Asking Appropriate Questions

Transformational Change Is Not A Straight Line – Who Benefits?

It is important to remember that there is both a continuum of degree of what already exists as well as emergence of totally new concepts in parallel, and nothing absolute in the forward progress of mankind. There are thus various changes, impacting diverse members of society differently. If you are most affected by income inequality, you will be more accepting of change as you strive for more income. You may not be comfortable with it, but you will even be urging change. In contrast, if you have a good salary and have no financial worries, you are comfortable with the status quo, and you may be very resistant to change. And, while the influences of change have impacted different segments of a population differently, throughout time, certain portions of the population have been particularly threatened by transformational change in our current times as a long period of privilege has supported White males who have obtained particular social and/or economic status.

Figure 1.4 Evolution of Humankind

Evolution of Humankind

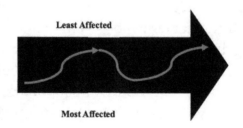

Even with privilege, to various degrees, people today are unhealthy financially, spiritually, physically and mentally. Personal debt and bankruptcy, and the decline of faith, religion, family and divorce impact the moral compass. Obesity, heart attacks, illness, all interconnect with depression, chemical dependency, and addiction.

Moving away from these conditions of self-image and self-centeredness to fulfillment and service, the outcome of happiness is redefined as giving more to life than you take as well as learning to co-create with others to help transform society in this time of historical transition. And with a shift from being human focused to being ecologically focused, we see a movement to connect with nature to better understand the environmental damage for which humans are responsible.

Making Connections Among New Ideas, People and Processes

Humans, beginning at the DNA level, are genetically wired to be in communion with one another. We are social creatures. Relationship and interactions are critical. This is a constant and the basis for emergence of new ways of thinking and developing "capacities for transformation."

At birth the learning clock begins. Instinct and intuition drive each baby to seek warmth, shelter and nourishment. Children are born with the need for human interaction, dependent on parents or caregivers. As the child grows s/he becomes more aware, learning all the while from their surroundings, environment and "teachers."

Empowering children with the ability to think, reason, discern and apply knowledge in a constantly creative context, is not only an enormous responsibility, but crucial for the survival of all. Our new challenge is to realize that each of the above abilities will need to be co-created within a "futures context" that will be very different from a traditional context.

Community and relationships are being reframed. In the

21st century, community and relationships are being redefined as physical, digital and cognitive capacities are rethought. There is much research and study on human growth and development from the prism of traditional thinking, but little on the impact of the digital domain. We are still in the transition and there has not been enough time to grow the body of transformational knowledge.

How Can We Educate the Whole Child?

A progression of learning for the 21st century strategically must focus on the whole child, body, soul and mind. The responsibilities of /for this human growth and development requires new thinking, innovative perspectives and transformational methods. How much can be left to chance? How much can be institutionalized? How much is left to individual choice? Transformational learning requires a holistic approach to all of these questions within a different context that involves anticipating what may emerge apart and in parallel from what has worked in the past.

How Do We Support Relationships?

An emerging important overarching question is: how does membership in a digital community, and/or virtual relationship, impact human growth and development? The issue of supporting relationships is especially problematic with the challenges presented by technology that include virtual relationships.

Michael Rosenfeld, Stanford University sociologist, has studied how our relationships have evolved over the past 80 years. Key findings of his research include:

- Since 1940, traditional ways of meeting partners – through family, in church and in the neighborhood – have all been in decline.
- A 2017 survey of American adults found that about 39

percent of heterosexual couples reported meeting their partner online, compared to 22 percent in 2009. Worldwide, it is estimated that revenues for matchmaking services will surpass $2.5 billion by 2024 (Statista, nd).

• Meeting a significant other online has replaced meeting through friends. People trust the new dating technology more and more, and the stigma of meeting online seems to have worn off.

So, the question then becomes how does this reframing of relationships impact "classroom" learning and selecting an appropriate teacher? How does this connect with future employability? It also brings into question how the traditional approach to learning in a classroom can transition to a more transformative "futures" approach that will be designed within the context of the emerging philosophy of "connectivism." In other words, is the advent of digital technology and the focus on interconnections and interdependency change the very nature of what historically has been seen as "education?"

How are Schools Aligned with Societal Expectations?

The 20th century desire for "instant gratification" has a potential not to be amplified in the 21st century. This social expectation for immediate results has impacted schools and our expectations of student achievement, accomplishment and the role of education in producing direct social benefits. Yet, despite the desire for efficiency and clear results of our activities, in the 20th century, frustration at NOT being able to achieve the expected conformity and definition of success many times resulted in shame, depression, fear and illness. These unhealthy conditions many times resulted in self-medication and escaping reality with a pharmaceutical answer through pills, narcotics and alcohol.

In the 20th century, an individual's attempt to address symptoms, without developing a sense of self was the response to adversity. This kind of response directly connects the "instant gratification" expectation for immediate results. The war on drugs and push for gun control never addressed root causes and therefore never found traction for fundamental changes to occur.

A 21st century expectation may be associated less with direct and immediate consequences and become more aligned with deeper meanings and connections. If you feel good about yourself, have grit, and exhibit a mental model of hope, choice, and achievement, your sense of identify will be strong and well founded. How might schools be aligned with these sorts of social expectations? How might education need to change to accommodate shifts in societal expectations?

Design Consideration #1 Learning is Continuous.

Communities of the Future will need a new mechanism/means to instill how to learn, birth to grave, in a constantly emerging, adaptable and flexible way that is financially sustainable and reflects the ability to co-create emergent transformative ideas in parallel to existing community beliefs.

Design Consideration #2 Learning How to Learn.

Foundational to achieving this is teaching the skills to learn, unlearn, and uplearn (the ability to think and function at a higher level of complexity), as well as be able to adapt and embrace new conditions and emerging perceptions and thinking. It means getting comfortable with rapid transformational change and having the ability to let go of previous mental models.

Design Consideration #3 Knowledge manipulation.

Going forward, crucial will be the ability, in near real time, to access, discern and connect knowledge across disciplines, in real world predictable and unpredictable situations. Essential to survival and the capacity to thrive will be the ability to recognize a futures context as it evolves and transforms as well as the ability to learn, unlearn, and uplearn. Creativity, imagination, collaboration and out-of-the-box thinking will be the tools for an adaptable future.

Design Consideration #4 Being digitally connected.

This means access to robust, reliable and affordable broadband internet is foundational. What must be addressed is the divide between those with economic stability and those economically unstable. Those unstable will be severely limited in their ability to access and participate economically and socially in the new emerging global society. They are at a disadvantage.

Design Consideration #5 Use of Time.

Humans + understanding/knowledge of Earth (natural resources, sciences, biology, physics, chemistry) + creativity of spirit = a transformed quality of life. As mankind invented and created laborsaving devices, the equation of time necessary for survival (work) decreased. Work was equated from all day, every day, sunup to sundown Monday through Saturday, to a 40 hour, Monday through Friday (8 hours a day) work week. Work was equated to time on task. Anything beyond the 8 hour or 40-hour work week was identified as "overtime."

This system design of time was applied to schools and learning. Time on task would equal to a predetermined amount of learning. The assessment of learning through a standardized test would be scored by the number of answers given, based on a predetermined outcome. This was an effective approach to human progress until the framework of a different kind of future began to emerge based on a society and economy that is increasingly interconnected and complex.

In the current education system, time is constant, with learning prescribed and limited. In the new Ecosystem of Learning, learning is constantly adapting to a transformation of new realities and connecting emergent ideas and methods in an apparent dance of timeless creations.

Building Parallel Processes

As we move through transition, historical industrial systems thinking applied to teaching and learning will coexist in parallel as the application of ecosystem thinking and structure is aligned to teaching and learning. Learning ecosystem design essentials will include parallel approaches that support new ways of approaching and valuing learning while also building on past successes and structures. Figure 1.5 below provides a summary of the parallel processes that will be needed to support transforming education in the 21st century.

Figure 1.5 Learning Ecosystem Parallel Processes

Learning Ecosystem Parallel Processes

Industrial Approach	Ecosystem Perspective
• Contained	• Creative
• Controlled	• Adaptive
• Predictable	• Permeable
• Scalable	• Dynamic
• Repeatable	• Systemic
• Measurable	• Self-correcting

Learning Ecosystem Design Essentials

A learning ecosystem embeds individuals and social structures within the context of the larger societal need for continuous transformation and openness to learning. There are several design essentials to a learning ecosystem, summarized below.

- **Mindflex**: Meaningful relationships connect learners. Social-Emotional Learning and Growth Mindflex is foundational. Mindflex is the ability to adapt to constant transformation and, as we use it, is more than a cognitive response.
- **Wholistic Learner:** Processes are in place to provide resources and learning experiences to meet individual student needs, in addition to discerning passions and abilities.
- **Creativity, Imagination & Curiosity:** Instruction is differentiated, focused on developing skills and attitudes of creativity, imagination, and curiosity.
- **Flexible & Adaptive Structures**: The structure of the educational system is flexible, adaptable and empowers students to take ownership in their learning.
- **Adaptive Curriculum**: Curriculum is constantly adapting in ways relevant to a different kind of future demanding deep levels of understanding and thinking within a futures context. Trans-literacy within a transformational context coupled with Science, Technology, Arts, Engineering and Math skills are foundational.
- **Equitable & Appropriate Use of Technology**: Equitable and systemic use of technology improves accessibility of information and enhances opportunities for learning. Especially as knowing and doing become augmented by technology, formal and informal learning ecosystems need to take advantage of these advances while attending to access and appropriateness.

- **Facilitation of Learning**: Professional Development models the expectations of classroom instruction by being data driven, differentiated, and at higher levels of thinking, and always within a futures context.
- **Telemetry**: Supporting lifelong learning and continuous learning in informal as well as formal settings, multiple kinds of measures of accomplishment need to be made available throughout the life span of individuals. This kind of data system supports dynamic, changing expectations and needs for learning and can take advantage of newer (blockchain, for example) technologies. Input is collected as a continuous process and a variety of data sources can be accommodated. This moves education away from the collection of easy-to-measure "data" as "indicators" of learning to 'telemetry" or ubiquitous ways of documenting and demonstrating learning.

Example: Learning in the Age of COVID

Below is a table that captures these different dimensions of a new learning ecosystem as they might be explored from a pre-COVID learning paradigm and as they might be explored from a post-COVID, ecosystem design approach.

Table 1.2 Learning in the Age of COVID Example

	Pre-COVID Learning Paradigm	Post-COVID Learning Paradigm
	Factory Model	**Small Learning Community**
Overriding Design Construction	Implementing the principles of assembly line manufacturing in education by standardizing curriculum, creating tracks, and minimizing variability within a class.	Maintain a learning community that integrates curriculum across subject areas, making transformational learning rigorous and relevant so that students graduate ready and prepared for high skill, 21st-century "uplearning" and employment.

	Order through Discipline	Personalized Environment
School Culture	Large factory model schools produce a culture that breeds anonymity, lack of ownership of the educational environment or their own learning. Crowd control is managed by bells, hall passes and suspensions that seek to control behavior	A transformational culture encourages active participation by students, parents and the community in the educational process. Diverse learning environments strive to empower students, treating them respectfully, as individuals, in an adult professional manner. (Differentiated Instruction)
	Memorization of Facts	**Authentic Learning and Assessment**
Curricular Goals	Expose students to a wide variety of topics and concepts in compartmentalized, unrelated, short-term experiences so that students can demonstrate mastery on content specific standardized tests or other measures of accomplishment.	In-depth exploring of concepts and themes that can be related to other contexts and situations to ensure that students can apply what they have learned at any time in any way. Infusion of 21st-century skills into the learning environment so that ALL teachers are responsible for the emergence of creative and connective learning.
	Teacher-Led Lessons	**Teacher-Facilitated Lessons**
Methods of Instruction	Teachers create discrete daily lessons that tend to be on the lower end of Bloom's Taxonomy (Sosniak, 1994). Students tend to work alone using the text as the primary resource.	Teachers work with students to create longer projects that engage students to become more active in their learning and that provide a context and application for new transformational knowledge and skills.
	Remediation and Instruction	**Collaboration and Integrations**
Use of Technology	Students use technology infrequently to do some web research, type reports, solve simple math equations. Some content systems are used for remediation or instruction	Technology/internet is seamlessly used to connect learners to seek and solve real world problems and emergent challenges.
	Autocratic Top-down Leadership	**Transformational Leadership**
Leadership Framework	Top-down direction coming from Federal and State mandates to Local School Boards. Local responses are reactive and not proactive. Perception of dislocation by local stakeholders.	All Stakeholders (including students) are empowered and encouraged to participate proactively in the learning community. As long as State and Federal mandates are honored, every effort is made to provide District direction that is crafted with broadbased community input. Contributions are honored, appreciated, and valued. This offers a new way to give parents and students an opportunity to be a part of the ongoing transformation.

Teaching and Learning at a 60,000-foot view

So much more is known today than at the turn of the last century. Because of technology, the Internet, and social media, mankind is connected and has moved from being self-dependent to globally interdependent. Manufacturing, making stuff, and the essentials of life are now dependent on global supply chains. Relationships and community once referred to a physical connection, now include an online, digital dimension. That being said, the concept of living in isolation no longer is viable, and through availability of high-speed broadband internet, a person can choose to live a lifestyle, and work anywhere on the planet and possibly in the future on other planets.

Brain research has discovered how the brain works and how it physically changes as a result of experiences and learning. Emerging research has mapped the brain and correlated growth and development with academic achievement. Paired with adaptive technology, physical limitations of hearing, seeing or movement can be overcome, allowing the learner to develop their intellectual capacity, expanding their ability to learn and create.

Teaching and Learning at 10,000 feet

Again, we need to look beyond the current, and upcoming turbulence, to what is on the other side. The rigidity of the 20th-century system of learning, specifically in the public schools, needs to be recast in 21st-century systems thinking. Conformity and standardization must give way to differentiated, personalized learning based on the learner's aptitudes, readiness and interest. Memorization of facts and regurgitation, multiple choice, fill in the blank tests must give way to the ability to access, manipulate and apply knowledge creatively to both real world predictable and unpredictable situations.

The ability to realize and adapt to change and context, coupled with the skill to think and discern, empowers the learner to learn, unlearn and uplearn constantly. Adaptability provides the learner the ability to reinvent themselves as conditions change, which encourages letting go of the mental model of "one and done" learning to learning that is constant and transformative. Learning, from birth to grave, are survival skills for prosperity and relevance in the reality of an ever-changing world.

Summary

This chapter explored key ideas necessary for transformational thinking as we transition and adapt to the challenges of the 21st century. Understanding and exploring human and social learning systems as continuously needing to undergo change, and challenging mindsets that have prevented change from occurring, this chapter explores transformational thinking from a futures or "mind-flex" perspective. The specific focus on formal education builds on the interconnected, symbiotic relationship of education and society. This chapter posits that the education system as it is now does not provide the experiences and opportunities for children to adapt to the future. And without having an education system that supports transformational ways of being, society similarly lacks the capacity to transition and emerge to meet the challenges and changes we are facing now and into the future.

The next chapter provides practical explorations of how to engage key stakeholders in the kinds of conversations necessary for transformational change to occur. Building on Communities of the Future (COTF, nd) strategies, the next chapter offers approaches to community transformation of schools that have been used in business and community settings.

Notes

Figure 1.2: Educational Conformity Visualized.

Accessed Mariam's Blog, 2013: https://mariamboutros2013.wordpress.com/2013/11/26/conformity-the-way-we-learned-to-live/

Figure 1.3 X-1 Plane.

This work has been identified as being free of known restrictions under copyright law, including all related and neighboring rights. You can copy, modify, distribute and perform the work, even for commercial purposes, all without asking permission. See Other Information below. https://creativecommons.org/publicdomain/mark/1.0/

Chapter 2

Futures Generative Dialogue

Futures generative dialogue engages all stakeholders in meaningful collaboration and discussion, focusing on existing mental models, opening thinking, and beginning the process of visioning what could be. Historically though, 20th century civilization has created hardened silos, sifting and sorting people by race, ethnicity, age, social class, education, profession and physical location. Not having meaningful interactions or relationships then has created stereotypes and intolerance of different perspectives.

Beginning with school structure, sorting children by chronological age or physical community membership, then continued forward with elderly warehoused in retirement communities, the opportunity to share life experiences and the responsibility to take care of one another is missed. This chapter explores how futures generative dialogue can be used to support this kind of intergenerational approach to community learning and transformation.

At this point in history, perhaps the question to be asked is what are we here for? How are we all to survive and flourish together in the next century? It is almost like we need to create adaptive structures, systems and experiences that constantly reprogram humanity with increasing emergent knowledge and empathy. Core mental models and beliefs need to evolve from an inward to an outward perspective.

Strategies For Futures Generative Dialogue

Finding Consensus and Getting Centered

At one point, almost every playground for children included a "merry-go-round." This was a play structure that was designed for children to get on, hold on, spin, and experience centrifugal force. Children learned that the faster the merry-go-round spun, and the closer one was to the edge, the harder it was to hang on. On the edge, it took lots of energy to hang on or stand up, the world passing by quickly and the energy pulling you off. As a result, it was hard to focus. Children learned that by moving to the center of the merry go round, forces were not as strong. With the merry-go-round continuing to spin, once centered and balanced, the child could stand up without holding onto the rings. And even though they were still spinning and subject to forces, they were better able to process their observations and hang on than they were when they were positioned "on the edge."

Figure 2.1 Merry-Go-Round Experiences

In thinking of a new process and system of learning, there needs to be a realization that the spinning will not stop. In moving away from the turbulent edge to the center, one can have a new perspective in which the previous challenge of just staying upright is replaced by a new perspective in which one can see reality differently and understand the need to build new "capacities" to prepare for a different kind of future. Part of getting centered in a newly emerging reality is moving away from chaos and moving ahead to "future basics."

As mankind has evolved and constantly prepared for a different kind of emergent future, new patterns in every area of society have emerged and become necessary, with each new civilization and culture constructed on new ideas and methods. The American experiment in democratic governance is just such an example.

Rethinking Fundamental Freedoms

The United States *Declaration of Independence* was written to proclaim fundamental, shared common beliefs that reflected a new theory of government. It was later followed by the framework of governance known as the Constitution. Historically, both documents have been accepted and supported by all Americans. The fact that increasingly large segments of our society, especially among the less educated and more fearful, are losing faith in our democracy and the ability of our society to provide for the "common good," challenges our ability to adapt to current historical challenges in the same way that our forefathers adapted to the needs of their times to ensure individual liberty and provide great promise for those often without rights in prior governance systems.

Several key concepts from these two documents are crucial starting points to becoming "centered" and building consensus in designing a system of learning appropriate to the new age that is emerging.

From the Declaration of Independence, equality, and the pursuit of life, liberty, and happiness must be foundational to the new educational design. Bringing meaning and making transformational concepts operational and effective in an age of constant change are vital to our ultimate civilizational goals and outcomes. The emerging system of learning must have equal access and be flexible to meet student needs. Building consensus of what "life, liberty and happiness" is in a 21st century that is constantly changing, interconnected and complex, needs to be defined and explored.

It needs to be noted that the U.S. Constitution was the operational framework within which to move forward the vision of government desired in the Declaration of Independence. It also needs to be noted that the desire was "to form a more perfect Union" and that the unfinished American experiment continues to be a work in progress. The question remains, how do these concepts need to be adapted in an emerging age very different from the past?

As the force of transformational change continues to propel us beyond the confines of a more constrained society and economy, the success in the design of a new system of learning that will support an "adaptable" society will need to be conceived from the middle looking out, not from the edge hanging on (reflecting on the metaphor of the playground merry-go-round). The fundamental nature of such a society will need to be able to keep its citizens connected and productive within the emergent system without being thrown off any transformed societal merry-go-round. Maybe there is a need for a *Declaration of Interdependence*.

What is needed is a new foundation of principles, policies, protocols and practices that are appropriate for a newly emerging society to include the ability to discern transformational abilities and aptitudes that are consistent with constant change.

It will reflect the ability to stay on a "global merry go round of transformation" without getting thrown off because capacities for transformation were not developed for the new and emerging society some call an "ecological civilization."

Just as our forefathers (and foremothers) often sacrificed their time, talent and money for the dream of a greater good in a time of historical transformation, we can expect no less from ourselves as we are propelled out of the Industrial Age into the unknown. As a result, many varied leaders at all levels and professions will need to be willing to help our global society prepare for a different kind of future and in so doing give more to life than one takes.

Asking the Right Questions

As we saw with transforming education, strategies for futures generative dialogue include not only asking the right questions, but learning how to listen *deeply*. Listening for value, connecting ideas and people, empathizing and looking for access points, and risking the unknown by challenging old patterns and exploring new ones are all transformational skills necessary for a futures generative dialogue.

Facilitating Interlocking Networks

Communities of the future strategies that support futures generative dialogue require opening up the spaces and encouraging participation for diverse perspectives, races, cultures, ethnicities and intersectionalities that can make a difference. To facilitate interlocking networks, futures generative dialogue does more than invite people to the table. It orchestrates conditions and environments to provide safety and sustainability for on-going and emerging relationships and explorations.

Facilitating interlocking networks also requires "letting go" and allowing networks to evolve, emerge, and develop meaningful collaborations organically. The issues of control, orchestration, outcomes, and goals actually are relinquished in support of emergence, relationship, and meaningfulness.

Global Communities

The COVID-19 pandemic has been a globally shared event that has touched every person and place on Earth. This significant emotional experience has caused all to stop, reflect, and now consider what comes next. It has accelerated change that was already occurring prior to the COVID outbreak, creating access points for new ideas and thinking.

As with the two mice characters, Him and Haw, from the book *Who Moved My Cheese?* (Johnson, 2015), some during the pandemic went looking for new cheese while others were paralyzed by fear and anger. The worldwide pandemic has impacted all communities across the globe and created this kind of uncertainty and challenge for individual and collective responses. Those who have had the courage to explore for new cheese, now have built capacity within themselves that if the cheese moves again, they are not afraid to risk and go searching. This is the essence of growth leading to the potential capacity of being a transformational thinker and doer.

New Normal

Designing for the new normal, change will be constantly shifting and moving faster as well as transforming continuously, if that is possible. To be effective in a world of transformation, education and learning will need to be designed to adapt and include the realization that everything is interconnected and constantly transforming. The ability to access, discern and connect emerging and existing knowledge across disciplines will ensure the potential to anticipate and deal with real world situations, both predictable and unpredictable.

Technological Innovation

Technology innovation will continue to reframe lifestyle, work, and the role of human beings. Communities and relationships, once defined by physical location, now digitally have a global dimension. Again, the common theme is the interconnectedness of humans with our physical, intellectual and biological environment.

As a citizen of the world, we need to navigate these changes to break old barriers. Like Chuck Yaeger, we need to find the courage to break through the turbulence and get to the other side.

Through The Looking Glass

Personal Reflection

Reflections from John: I consider myself to be very lucky to have known my great-grandmother, Juanita Delbridge. Nena, to us kids, was married at 20, a World War I widow with a child at 21, who went on to become a teacher, and later a principal in Edmund, Oklahoma. Living to be 100 years old, Nena experienced many educational reforms, including moving from the one-room schoolhouse to the "modern" industrial model, consolidated town school that sifted and sorted children by age, race, standardized instruction and measured academic with assessments that required the memorization of stuff. Teaching and learning was institutionalized.

Visiting my classroom in the fall of 1984 when I was a teacher, she told me that during my professional career, teaching and learning would evolve yet again and challenged me to help facilitate it. Her hope, when the change happened, was that teaching would go back to the one-room schoolhouse model, where learning was exciting and fun, and where kids were clustered by their abilities, not their age. Is it possible that our digital world can connect us in a learning environment in which we will be able to interact with each other as "learning networks" similar to the principle of a one-room schoolhouse using the principles of "connectivism."

Reform, Transform, or Both?

As we move into the 21st century, it is important to discern what patterns from the last 100 years should go forward and what new patterns should be embraced. At the core, every institution, social belief, commerce, governance and spiritual persuasion is in a state of transformative change. Power structures that have been in place for 100 years are evolving. Those who have been in power are fearful of losing it and therefore resist change, pushing back against any new idea that will challenge the comfort of traditional ideas and methods.

Just like Major Yeager breaking the sound barrier, it must be acknowledged there will be extreme turbulence as we transit from old to the new. But it should also be remembered that like the caterpillar morphing into the butterfly, it will be totally different on the other side.

No one knows now what society and the world will look like on the other side of the "transformation barrier." Individuals are discovering trends and weak signals (potential minitrends and trends when they first appear) that give us insights into the future but in no way can predict or control what things may become. Connecting and sharing these discoveries with others sharpens our insights of what could, might or should emerge in a future.

Emerging new norms, perspectives, and realties come with multiple barriers, push back, and apprehensions. It is appar-

ent that flexibility, adaptability and open Mindflex are design essentials not found in 20th century beliefs, structures, institutions and systems, and particularly not public education.

To get from where we are, to where we need to be, especially when we don't know where to be or go in a constantly changing world, will mean continuing with present practices as new ones emerge, are designed, embraced, accepted and made operational in parallel. Status quo and transformational change will need to coexist at the same time as transition occurs.

Over the last century, the United States has moved and committed to an economy based on consumption and excess. Demand for affordable products, coupled with increases in wages, often prices the blue-collar United States workforce out of the market. Moving manufacturing jobs to underdeveloped countries, with lower wage costs, has created an economic paradox. American demand for consumer goods continues to be high, but to keep the costs down, has meant moving jobs offshore. As a result, American middle-class workers are losing their jobs. Compounding the problem are generations who have been conditioned not to fix or wear out but throw away and buy the next great thing......and if you can't afford it, buy on credit.

The call for more in the 20th century has produced people who are unhealthy financially, spiritually, physically and mentally. When personal debt and bankruptcy are coupled with the decline of faith, religion, family and divorce along with obesity and heart attacks, all interconnect to create depression, chemical dependency, and addiction. These are symptoms of an increasingly unhinged society.

The founding fathers of the United States established foundational beliefs that all men are created equal and endowed by their Creator with unalienable Rights, to include Life, Liberty and the Pursuit of Happiness. Over time, "men" was expanded to include all people, regardless of sexual orientation, race, gender, ethnicity, or national origin. Later, the Constitution established a framework and structure to work towards, and make operational, the beliefs laid out in the Declaration of Independence. As a global society we continue to evolve to create more equitable opportunities for all as part of a transformative process.

Communities of the future must face, address and transform beyond the following challenges in education and as a society:

- We no longer live as isolated individuals or groups. We are globally interdependent and as such must have the capacity for cultural respect and empathy. Our social well-being and economic survival are dependent on this.
- Academic growth, learning and the acquisition and application of knowledge is no longer confined to a single physical space. Virtual reality, and the ability for video conferencing, frees learners from a specific time and place to real time teachable moments and or on demand lessons, from anywhere on the planet with a digital internet connection.
- In addition, society must learn to see past a person's

physical attributes, to appreciate and value their creativity and intellectual abilities, not how they look and dress.

- There must be a realization and discernment between wants and needs. The school experience needs to distill and truthfully connect how income impacts life choices.
- It needs to be emphasized that the world ecosystem is fragile and has finite resources that must be safeguarded.
- It is imperative that we acknowledge the imperfections of the United States and that we reflect on the right to life, liberty, and pursuit of happiness for all globally and not exclusively to Americans.

TEACHING, LEARNING, SCHOOL & SOCIETY

"I am not living to work; I am working to live so I can enjoy my husband, my son, and my life."

—Tabitha Carver

The concept of school, and the continuum and sequence of formal and informal learning throughout the lifespan, need always to focus on the learner, thus reinforcing a system of learning that adapts to the child, not the child adapting to the system. Each learner needs to be looked at individually and holistically, with a balanced focus on body, soul and mind. If learning is taken in its widest interpretation as what individuals and society do to maintain growth and adaptive capabilities, there are various ways to rethink learning beyond the traditional classroom.

Stage one, what once was labeled elementary school, focuses to be on how to learn to include:

- The ability to read, discern and apply what was read.
- Communicate and express thinking in multiple strategies (orally, visually, writing, digitally)
- social mobility
- character/mindflex development
- math and pattern learning
- social cohesion and social equality.
- "60,000 foot" 21st-century learning tenets

Stage two, which was once labeled Middle School, focus would reinforce and build on Stage One tenets but go forward and explore and support student self-discovery and advocacy, including

- identifying passions, abilities, skills and aptitudes;
- addressing biological, social, emotional and developmental needs, especially for traditional middle-school aged students who are developing new forms of reasoning and identity and experiencing tremendous hormonal and body growth differences, also impacting their emotions and their thoughts which are becoming more internal and complex;
- developing moral perspectives that support emergent and diverse possible futures; and
- connecting passions to professions and aptitudes along with respect for all professions and life choices.

Stage three, formally high school and informally, beyond high school: the deliberate reinforcement of the undergirding tenets of stage one and two in order to build upon identified passions and abilities from stage two. The goal would be to craft a realistic launch plan into the world and always anticipate what is next. To discern what a realistic lifestyle would be, individuals at this stage of their educational and moral development, would connect individual passions with professions in order to envision what their desired contributions to the world could be.

Figure 2.2 What Kind of Work Do You Do?

"It is not what company am I going to work for, it's what new jobs am I going to create?"

The Countdown And The Launch

It is clear that reforming current 20th century learning practices to fit 21st-century realities is not realistic, and that transformational change and new mental models at both educational and social levels are needed to launch this futures rocket ship. Humankind is emerging from a self-imposed historical cocoon and must have the courage to overcome the paralyzing 20th-century avoidance of risk in order to see the new. This time of historical transition is a time of exploration and discovery.

Asking appropriate questions, and then listening to the responses, unveils new perspectives and possibilities. These new insights and perspectives, shared, connected, and dialogued with others brings into focus the mosaic of a new normal. It identifies entry points and structures into the new normal. It reveals connections from the past, to now, to what is next.

As we move into the 21st century, accelerating change will be constant with challenges and solutions that cannot be viewed in isolation, but holistically, due to the fast pace of interdependent change. Meeting the "what is next" means a realization that all is interconnected, and like touching a spider's web, every action and decision sends out ripples and impacts others.

As a result, rethinking the concept of learning in a world of constant and transformational change, a new system of transformational learning will be required. We are at the beginning of a new dawn. The butterfly is emerging, but not fully free of the cocoon. The wings have not yet unfolded, dry, and ready for flight. Just as the butterfly is realizing its place in the new environment of a constantly changing 21st-century, education, learning and teaching is doing the same.

With the rocket already on the pad and ready for launch, the following chapters will extend these initial perspectives of change to further problematize how societal change is possible. Rethinking our past, exploring possible, plausible and desirable futures, inventing and organizing around new societal core metaphors and values, and developing strategies to work together, synergistically and globally to meet the challenges of the future are strategies on this path of transformation. Building capacities and understandings for transformational leaders in this new ecosystem will be vital to support these efforts and will be the focus of the final chapters of the book.

Notes

Figure 2.1 Merry-Go-Round Experiences.
https://proplaygrounds.com/product/classic-commercial-merry-go-round/ This image was originally posted to Flickr by kristinafh at https://flickr.com/photos/22298014@N07/2522949288. It was reviewed on 6 February 2022 by FlickreviewR 2 and was confirmed to be licensed under the terms of the cc-by-2.0.

Figure 2.2 What Kind of Work Do You Do?
https://pxhere.com/en/photo/1132526?utm_content=shareClip&utm_medium=referral&utm_source=pxhere The image is released free of copyrights under Creative Commons CC0. You may download, modify, distribute, and use them royalty free for anything you like, even in commercial applications. Attribution is not required.

Chapter 3

Learning in Transition

Introduction

Personal Reflection

In early 2020, before the pandemic was really understood, I (JF) was in Italy writing and researching about learning transformations. I walked the ruins of ancient Rome, the Agora, and the halls of the Vatican. I rented an apartment in Florence with friends, and embarked on daily trips to The Academy, the Uffizi, and Pisa, among other notable places. My goal was not to check off these amazing tourist sites, however, but to embrace the spirit of transitional Italy of the early 13th through 15th centuries. This spirit was in evidence as I walked by the University on the way to the Leaning Tower of Pisa, roughly along the same path that Galileo took as he conducted gravity experiments. I walked the same streets as Michelangelo and saw the church where he did his cadaver dissections in the basement, and I spent time at the Academy where his famous statue, The David, is housed. I walked into medieval and Renaissance churches, including the Cathedral of Florence built in the 13th–15th centuries with the prominent 24-hour gravity clock with time progressing "backwards" from sunset to sunset.

These physical spaces and manifestations of human ingenuity reflected the shifting social and political *Zeitgeist*, literally the "time ghost" of a society in transition. In contrast to the ancient sites and rituals I observed in Rome, in Florence and Pisa I could sense the birth of the modern era and see the seeds of transformation, now, coming to fruition in our modern society.

The coincidence of leaving Italy late in February, 2020, just as the spread of COVID-19 was becoming critical in northern Italy, and returning to the US where we were faced with the beginnings of our own epidemic response and political turmoil, emphasized the life-cycles of societies. From the pandemic of the 13th- and 14th-century Europe to the world-wide pandemic in 2020. From the birth of science, philosophy and art that brought light and discipline to the world, now pushing boundaries of what it means to be human in the 21st century with artificial intelligence and cyborgs. From the assumption of risk and demonstration of bravery in the face of pushing the boundaries of societal mores by pioneers like Galileo and Michelangelo to Black Lives Matter, conspiracy theories and fake news. Are these cycles repeating, or spaced as the life-cycles of societal epochs marking key transformations to entirely new ways of thinking and being? Have we extinguished the possibilities of the 500-year cycle of the Renaissance as we stand at the doorstep of our next (and hopefully not last) cycle of humanity on this planet?

Standing at the Precipice

We are standing on the precipice of societal transformation, looking to a future that will be very different than the present and past. We are at the cusp of change that is unprecedented in human history. With technological advances that include mobile communications, artificial intelligence, 3-D printing, genetic mapping and genome editing, social media, virtual reality, artificial organs, bionic prosthetics, nanomedicine, quantum computing, facial recognition and other biometric identification strategies, robotics, and Global Positioning Systems (GPS), we are more connected, more interdependent, more aware of the challenges, differences, and concerns across the world and have more capability to shape the course of the human race than ever before. Computing and technological advances have accelerated the pace of change and promoted innovations that were not even imagined a century ago. A single cell phone has more computing and communication power than most of the equipment used for our first space exploration missions in the 1960s.

These scientific advancements have generated new ethical dilemmas and concerns about what it means to be human. We can genetically modify embryos to prevent future diseases, deformities, and other human maladies but, should we use CRISPR to create the "perfect" human? Implantations replace damaged body parts and nanotechnologies enhance bodily responses, potentially creating new capacities and abilities for humans. When do we cross the line from helping amputees with better protheses to creating the next cyborg with superhuman capabilities? Artificial intelligence has advanced to the extent that machines have the capacity to learn, create and problem solve. AI has evolved from programmed simulations of learning to create learning machines. When do learning machines make humans irrelevant? And what, then, does it mean to be human? Advances in telecommunications allow for virtual meetings, musical performances, and community development, accelerated during the COVID-19 pandemic. And virtual reality creates interactions and supports experiences without ever leaving home. Will we come to the point where we don't ever need to interact with each other face-to-face again? Will a world of work even be necessary as technologies become more advanced and capable of performing many human tasks?

These advances in technology, medicine, social media, among others, have implications for what it means to know and learn. We are living in times of constant change and transformation impacting every sector of society. What kind of learning do we need to survive in this kind of world? What does learning and knowing even mean in our current contexts and for survival in the future? Why might rethinking what it means to know and do, and think and learn, be important to better meet the challenges of the next epoch of human existence on this planet or others!?

This chapter will explore the question of what it means to learn during this particular transitional period leading to the next transformational epoch of human life on earth., building on the ideas of transformational thinking as a precursor to societal-level change. It will explore the learning ecosystem for its potential to prepare and shape humans to advance our world.

The Third Rail

Personal Reflection

I (Jayne) had an especially poignant moment when I was teaching computer science and mathematics that has stuck with me for the rest of my teaching and administrative careers. I had a young man who was taking both my high school pre-calculus class and my computer programming class. Even though I thought I was a pretty innovative mathematics teacher by introducing historical and technological innovations in the foundations of mathematics, I still organized my lessons as most of you have probably experienced mathematics classes. I would have a clear objective for every class. We would begin class with questions about homework, perhaps doing a few problems in class or even grading homework papers together. I would introduce a new topic and either model the problem-solving approach or assign groups to work on a problem that would demonstrate the concept or skill being taught. More homework would be assigned, and we would pretty much repeat the process the next day. I would spend all weekend developing lesson plans for the week and selecting rich problems that would demonstrate the concepts or processes we were learning. I had a clear idea where each class would end up and a clear understanding about how concepts would unfold and come together by the end of the year.

In my computer science class, I didn't have this same sense of control, understanding, or final destination. Teaching computer science in the 1980s, I was making the path as I went. In my computer programming classes, I would think of a really interesting problem that could be solved many different ways with options and suggestions for additional add-ons to the assignment. For example: *Develop a computer interface to play the gambling card game of 21. If you want, include options for betting and keeping track of money.* Or, for advanced data handling concepts, *Design an airport queuing system that will safely land airplanes but that can accommodate a disaster.* Or finally, for the introductory class: *Create a text reading program that will count the number of words in any text that I will then input.* (My test text would always be the Gettysburg Address – by the way, it has 62 words.)

These assignments, in the 1980s, were not necessarily straightforward using BASIC or PASCAL programming languages at the time. I would give the students these problems, THEN teach them the control structures they might need to accomplish the tasks. So how do you get textual input? What is a word? How do you get the computer to recognize words? How do you use a random number generator to simulate rolling dice? What kinds of data structures allow for artificial decision making in a crisis situation?

This one particular student came to me one day and asked, "Why don't you teach mathematics more like you teach computer programming?" I asked him what he meant. He explained that in mathematics, I was well-organized, methodical, thorough, but routine. They didn't really have to think. In computer science, I gave them interesting problems and let them wrestle with them for several days or weeks. **It wasn't obvious at the beginning of the lesson what they were going to need to do to solve the problem and often times they needed to try different things before a solution would occur. They could brainstorm strategies and share their failures and programs with others in class, learning from each other. There was not the expectation that they all did the same thing** and, in fact, they worked hard to do things differently than others. They developed their own programming styles and interests. And they immediately applied what we were learning to create programs that solved interesting problems.

I did change how I taught mathematics, at least to the extent that I could within the expected curriculum. More importantly, **this was the seed of doubt that has grown throughout these many years since into a tree of skepticism about what we think is really important about learning.** This was the third rail of an electric train system, the lethal one that is ignored but always there. This was the assumed way of things that needed to be exposed, challenged and disrupted.

Seeds of Doubt

This tree of doubt has grown with its own litany of questions. Why do we expect everyone to get the same thing out of formal learning activities? How do we accommodate interest? When do we learn prerequisites for future learning, or when can we save learning for as-needed experiences? How do nonformal and informal learning opportunities guide understandings about futures learning needs and opportunities? We no longer need to be walking encyclopedias. Information is readily accessible at any time or place.

At a societal level, these same seeds of doubt have been spread with questions about unmet expectations, conflict, and uncertainty. Why have our social safety nets let so many people fall through? Why can't we talk across political, economic, racial, and gendered lines? How do we prepare for a future that is so uncertain? Will our planet even be able to sustain human life in the near future?

The next section will explore some of the assumptions about formal, informal, and nonformal education that are maladaptive for learning in the current transformational period. These are captured by examining the underlying and often times unspoken myths we have about learning, the third rails that end up being lethal.

Learning Myths

Much of what we think counts as knowledge and the relationship we believe exists between knowing and learning is based on myths about societal needs and individual capacities that may no longer be viable. Myths, like metaphors, have a life cycle. At first, a social myth is told, as a story, and maintains its status as a story. As myths become more ingrained in a society, however, they lose their myth-like qualities and we fail to recognize them as myths, at all. They take on the appearance of underlying reality. **During transitional times, especially as our society is now experiencing, it becomes important to articulate and expose these myths in order to replace them with new ways of thinking.** Many of these myths served as the basis of support to maintain the mechanisms of modern society and were important at one time but now need to be explored and challenged for their validity and usefulness during transformational times. These myths will be explored in this chapter from social/economic perspectives as well as individual learning and schooling viewpoints.

Social/Economic Learning Myths

One of the most prevalent social myths about modern society that impacts our understandings about learning and influences how we engage children and adults in learning opportunities is the **myth of individual autonomy and accomplishment**. Students are rewarded in school, and workers are rewarded in the workplace, for individual achievement and success. Scholarships, awards, and raises are presented to the "best", however that is determined. We celebrate the GOAT—Greatest of All Times, and emulate those who have performed with individual distinction. We hold up our GOATs as exemplars for our children with subliminal messages that they, too, should strive for individual achievement and distinction.

The myth of individual accomplishment is ingrained in the democratic ideal as represented in the myth of Horatio Alger. This myth suggests that through hard work and preparation, and some luck, anyone can achieve success. Success, in this case, is typically tied to financial success and wealth that supports independence and autonomy. Being your own boss is the apex of individual accomplishment. This ideal of self-sufficiency gets translated to the value that, through education and hard work, anyone can pull themselves up "by their bootstraps." It also emphasizes individual accomplishment and progress in formal learning environments with the expectation that students need to demonstrate individual and independent mastery.

Our democratic principles evolved from the sixteenth century religious Reformation ideas of rejection of authority and emphasis on independent thinking and individually reasoned decision making. It is no coincidence that the rejection of papal rule occurred at the same time that advances in science and creative discovery ushered in the Renaissance with values for reasoning, empirical knowledge, new standards of beauty and societal and technological advancements. **Underlying this combined Renaissance Enlightenment was an emphasis on progress and a celebration of the individual.**

A focus on progress at societal and individual levels is the next societal myth that influences our ideas about learning. The **myth of progress** supports the ideas of the importance of the accrual of knowledge and advancement of society by expecting each generation to know more, do more, and accomplish more than the last. Associated with the myth of progress is the idea that formal learning implies the accrual of knowledge. Formal education has played a crucial role in conveying past information and knowledge for individual and societal advancement. By the late 19th century, and with the advent of the industrial revolution, societal progress was understood to require an educated populace who could assume their place in the march toward ever increasing technological, economic and scientific growth. Formal educational practices and structures evolved out of the need for education to serve as the handmaiden to economic and societal progress. Bells between classes were introduced to prepare students to become workers where bells signified the beginning and ending of work. The curriculum was laid out to provide a basic level of literacy and numeracy to ensure workers could continue to support more complex work situations, expectations and needs. Progress, as accrual, gets replaced in transformational times by recursive, dynamical, organic metaphors, as will be described later.

The **myth of competition** has guided society for the past 500 years and is implied in strategies for success, achievement and autonomy. This underlying value suggests there are winners and losers, and that it is much better to win than to lose. Implicit in this myth is the idea that those who "rise to the top" are like "fine cream" to be celebrated and valued. Along with the myths of autonomy and accomplishment, learning to "be" something is important to take one's place in society and, in so doing, to "rise to the top" of your profession or workplace. Academic accomplishment and credentials have been important in distinguishing who rises to the top and can compete for the best jobs, highest incomes, and most authority. Advanced degrees and credentials have made individuals in the modern era more competitive and provide a leg up for future success. As will be described below, collaboration, cooperation, and self-fulfillment take on new meanings in transformational times.

Finally, related to the myth of competition is the **myth of consumerism** that suggests more is better. Like the myth of progress, the myth of consumerism emphasizes continuous growth of the economy and production of consumer goods and services. Our economy is based on individuals having disposable incomes, and success and status are demonstrated by the quantity and quality of stuff that we own. Consumerism, as it underlies modern society, is intimately tied to competition and wealth which are, in turn, associated with learning. As will be described below, alternatives to consumerism support emergent economies and metrics that go beyond the accumulation of wealth as the goal.

These myths impact the value, need, and purpose for education and subsequent expectations for how we teach and the kind of learning that we value. With an emphasis on formal education, there are additional myths about learning that may no longer be viable in transformational times. These myths will be discussed below.

Educational Myths

The first educational myth that has impacted how we view learning and influenced expectations for individual learners is the **myth of the average**. Todd Rose (2016) wrote in his book, *The End of Average*, how the US Air Force tried to design the perfect fighter jet cockpit in the 1950s by designing for the average pilot. They took measurements of over 4000 pilots on 10 different metrics such as height, weight, torso length, and arm span. Analyses later showed that even across only three measures, less than four percent of pilots fell within the expected average ranges found in their design. What they determined was that they, in fact, failed to design for the average pilot because the average pilot does not exist. What they concluded was the **need for a more adaptive design**. Yet we continue to use average as a way of measuring students' learning. How far above average or below average are you? How does your score equate to a letter grade? How do you measure up? No one wants to be below average, but by its very nature, half of us will be!

The concept of average is a fairly recent mathematical concept applied to human endeavors. Before the modern era, it would not have made sense to anyone to know the average number of children in US households is 1.8 children. How do you have eight-tenths of a child? Once we developed the notion of average, we could develop more sophisticated statistics such as standard deviations and percentile scores. We make assumptions about the "normal" curve of student achievement and calculate where along this curve students fall. But just as Rose described with the study of pilots, there is no average student, and the assumption of normalcy may be an error. But the notion of average is so pervasive during the modern era that it is hard to imagine schooling without it.

For example, the idea of average is closely associated with

intelligence. The Intelligence Quotient (IQ) construct and test were developed during WWI to identify soldiers for leadership training. The IQ test is a test of quantitative reasoning and pattern recognition, skills useful for officers in WWI. This test, however, signifies only one dimension of intelligence. Yet the areas that are emphasized by this test, namely mathematics and logical and spatial reasoning, hold privileged status in the curriculum and in our understandings about intelligence. "Oh, you're good at math. You must be smart!" Or "Why would you want to major in English when you are so good at math and could get a good job!" The myth of average has provided ways of measuring and ranking intelligence that also privileges mathematical and logical thinking as exemplars of intelligence. The myth of average forces us to narrow our definitions of what knowledge is of most value and measure everyone against that same metric – assumptions that we will see are maladaptive in complex times where diversity, adaptation and transformation are key.

Because mathematics and logical thinking have become the exemplars of intelligence and are positioned at the pinnacle of valued knowledge, another myth of learning prevalent during the modern era is the **myth of right answers.** Even in non-quantitative learning, we look for "right answers" and conformity. We learn to do a five-paragraph essay. We follow the rules of grammar and convention in communicating in formal settings. We expect tasks and solutions to problem solving to be judged by standards of efficiency. By the time most students are in fourth or fifth grade, they learn that to be successful in school, you need to do things the way the teacher wants them. You risk ridicule or bad grades if you deviate from the expected. By middle school, where social pressures go well beyond the expectations of the teacher, you learn to avoid learning risks by going out on any proverbial academic limbs. Those who don't follow the academic and social rules of right answers, correct procedures, and risk avoidance suffer the consequences of humiliation and ostracism. Even with the occasional push from teachers who support creativity and ingenuity, there is always the standard of the "right answer" to be compared against.

The myth of right answers also has an implicit myth of **either/or logic** that makes difference undesirable. It is either A or B, not both. If you don't do A, then you have to justify why B is an alternative. The myth of right answers suggests one path, one way. And once that way is set, you have to be prepared to defend any deviation from it.

The myth of right answers is supported by the **myth of learning units.** Especially in formal learning settings, learning is broken down and organized in a "logical" way. These learning projections or sequences are roped together like kindergarteners on an outing holding a rope. The curriculum is broken down into bite-sized pieces and educational research explores the best way to organize these learning units for maximum learning outcomes. These empirical explorations of the "best" pathways through the desired curriculum are based on earlier assumptions about what knowledge is of most worth, and the myth of the average that suggests we can "average" learning to know which pathways produce the greatest learning outcomes.

The myth of learning units also has an implied **myth of assessment** that emphasizes we can assess learning by assigning numbers to it. What gets assessed, then, is that which can be quantified. In the world of assessment, all that counts for the assessment hammer are the nails of numbers. Everything that counts, has to be reduced to a number. If a learning opportunity cannot be measured in a way that reduces it to a number, we ignore it. A student's love of mathematics isn't a factor in whether the student receives an "A" grade. Career capability surveys designed to assess skills and the best occupations one might be suited for are based on the myth of assessment as well as a consumer myth that treats students like commodities to be consumed by society, emphasizing finding the most productive workplace or slot for an individual student. **The myth of assessment is maladaptive for a world of constant change and emergent strategies for preparing for change.** As discussed later, the myth of assessment has a very different relationship with the future than more adaptive approaches.

Educational interventions, including schools and teachers, are evaluated based on measures that can be put into a formula so comparisons can be made. This leads to a more recent myth, the **myth of accountability.** Schools are graded according to student test scores and other measurable outcomes such as student attendance, student discipline, and the percentage of students who receive free and reduced lunches. Teachers are evaluated based on how well their students perform on standardized tests, and teacher preparation programs are ranked based on how their former students are ranked as teachers, even though the only teachers that get ranked for these accountability measures teach tested subjects like mathematics and English. Just like the myth of average, we have created entire measurement systems and accountability industries to compare and distinguish, separate and celebrate without perhaps having captured anything of real value as we transition to our next epoch of human society.

The figure below captures the relationship among the social and educational myths as they have impacted our ideas about learning. The social expectations and views of individual autonomy and success, with an unending drive towards progress supported through competition and consumerism have especially impacted our formal systems of education, building on the myth of the average to constrain learning for right answers into learning units that can be checked off, measured and compared.

Figure 3.1 Social and Educational Myths

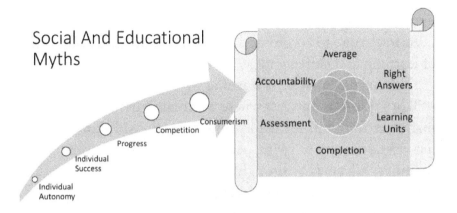

We have come to a place in public education where the drive towards and fulfillment of these myths has called into question our very purpose and future viability as educators preparing children and adults with necessary skills and dispositions to survive in our changing world. We see this especially in formal education where the myths that have focused our efforts may not support the kind of learning needed in these current transformational times.

One place to look for guidance in our understanding of social structures designed to facilitate learning is in the realm of pervasive learning. Pervasive learning, especially as it exists in nonformal and informal learning will be explored to provide insights for the future of learning and shifting roles for educators to support learners.

Pervasive Learning

Formal learning, as found in schools and training programs has been the focus of much of our discussion about learning. But informal and nonformal learning opportunities are becoming more prevalent due to the Internet and are important for understanding how our social and educational structures may need to change to accommodate and support these other ways of learning and shifting ideas about learning.

Nonformal learning is learning we engage in to learn a new skill or explore an interest where we are not driven by grades or mandates found in formal learning situations. Taking a cooking class, learning to swim, participating in non-mandated job trainings, advancing through the Boy/Girl Scout ranks, engaging in an information scavenger hunt in a history museum are examples of nonformal learning opportunities to pursue interests and enrich our lives. While there is an overlap with formal learning, nonformal learning typically takes place on a voluntary basis in public settings and is a component of life-long learning.

Informal learning is self-directed, tacit, and even incidental learning that occurs through experience or is driven by specific contexts. This kind of learning is typically unplanned and unstructured. It is often driven by curiosity and interest and can lead to nonformal and formal learning as interest and expertise grow. Examples of informal learning include looking up information on the internet because you wonder how the drink you are having at dinner is made, finding out who the sixth Brady child was in the TV series *The Brady Bunch*, and exploring how many times the Triple Crown in US horse racing has been awarded. Informal learning can also include looking up how to fix your toaster or set up your new computer, which may then lead to nonformal learning.

Informal and nonformal learning are important for **life-long learning**. With technology and the ready access to information, informal and nonformal learning are becoming more ubiquitous and important. And because we are so interconnected, pervasive access to information and people creates hyper-connectivity across space and time. We do not need a middle school class on how to fix small appliances but can look it up on YouTube when we need to know how to trouble shoot why our coffee isn't coming out warm and learn how to replace the heating element on our specific coffee maker model. We can directly contact our favorite thought leaders or authors and engage in conversations with them through venues such as Twitter. We can find old classmates and keep track of family and friends on Facebook and other social media sites. And we can meander through the internet to explore new ideas and concepts, comparing diverse perspectives and making connections among ideas, people and cultures.

Pervasive learning in our information rich, quickly changing world not only supports lifelong learning but requires specific lifelong learning skills and practices that take advantage of technologies and virtual access to people, ideas, and information. Pervasive learning shifts our needs to know beyond knowing "what," to knowing "about", knowing "how" and knowing "why." We can dig as deeply as we want into why things work the way they do or what exists in the larger world beyond our immediate contexts. **Pervasive learning also supports creativity and curiosity**. We become curious about how many horses have won the Triple Crown or why cicadas only come out every seventeen years. Technology supports our creative desires to know and encourages creativity. Not only can we become more creative with technology-in-hand, but because of the Internet, we can also see the products of others, further spurring our creative drive. TikTok is a case in point. People have become "influencers" because of their ability to post videos to the internet that shape opinions, trends and creative products.

Pervasive learning, supported by and existing because of technology, has created a society that is no longer complacent to have knowledge and ideas force-fed and determined by others. Connectivism, is a learning theory developed by George

Siemens that conveys how pervasive learning is facilitated by technology and learning networks. Like the World Wide Web, learning evolves as more and more connections are made. Learning is interest driven rather than content focused, and deeper because tangents and connections can be explored and expanded upon.

While the Reformation rejected the authority of the Pope and emphasized the importance of individuals having access to information in order to make up their own minds about scripture and interpret meaning, pervasive learning has provided for the free flow of information and ideas that goes even further in disrupting knowledge authorities in all aspects of human experience. **Discernment of information and critical judgment of truth,** whether existing and perceived as absolute or emergent and relative, now have become key skills in our transformational society where the latest conspiracy theories can spread like wildfire through the internet. Suspicion of information places new demands on how truth is defined as well as guidance for civil action.

The figure below suggests there are lessons to be learned from how we go about learning in the informal learning realm. The increased emphasis on and facilitation of nonformal and informal learning also provides guidance for how we can use pervasive learning opportunities to support formal learning and confront the learning myths that have rendered much of formal education meaningless, maladaptive, and contrary to learning needs in a rapidly changing, technology infused, dynamic, connected, transformational society.

Figure 3.2 Lessons from Informal Learning

Lessons from Informal Learning

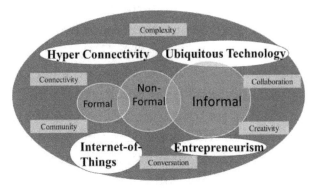

What we have learned about informal learning is that it is contextual, connected and often conversational. Small social groups get into debates about some fact or event and pull out their phones to look up information to support their claims or find out about some event. There is no need to be the smartest person in the room with a memory for facts and details – anyone can look up information to make connections and contribute to the conversation. We connect with these facts within contexts, creating new meanings and relationships among learning and supporting new understandings. Sometimes these internet explorations are short-lived, but other times, they prompt even deeper explorations and connections. Oftentimes, they lead us to contrary information and ideas requiring judgment and discernment.

Especially during the COVID-19 pandemic, we have seen how technology has facilitated collaboration and supported online communities. While many are experiencing "Zoom-fatigue" with too many online meetings, the skills of informal learning and connections in virtual environments have supported the needs for community, communications and collaboration.

We are also seeing a shift in our economy to support entre-preneurism and community transformation because of the ease of distribution of and access to information. The emergence of virtual concerts, support for informal food distribution strat-egies, and creative solutions to address human needs during crises are examples of informal social learning and networking that are supported by pervasive and connected learning and the desire of many to be a part of caring and compassionate com-munities of action. Age and experience are replaced by passion and vision as we see numerous examples of children reaching out to make a difference. This kind of entrepreneurism creates a new kind of economy that, while on the one hand, may have traditional economic impacts, goes further into **economies of social effect, influence and transformative change**.

Issues of increased connectivity, ready access to information, emergence of online communities, and focus on conversation-al exploration for community good, provide the basis of per-vasive, connected learning. Pervasive nonformal and informal learning that builds the capacities for transformational change is just beginning to have an impact on traditional approach-es to schooling and is quickly making traditional approaches to knowledge conveyance outdated, outmoded, and obsolete. Rather than thinking of the curriculum as maps of knowledge domains, pervasive learning offers new insights into how we might structure formal settings to better accommodate the kind of learning and passions needed for true transformation of our society.

One image of how formal learning can be impacted by per-vasive information and ubiquitous technology is to think about domains of learning from the geologic perspective of **learning contours.** Traditional **curriculum maps** visually display the learning standards for a subject or grade to include learning outcomes, competency levels, and instructional sequencing.

The expectation of a curriculum map is that everyone proceeds across the matrix of competencies and skills to ensure "coverage" of the predefined content. A child cannot proceed to the next grade or learning unit until the competencies as mapped have been satisfied and typically demonstrated through some measured activity like a test.

Visualize the difference between a curriculum contour and a curriculum map as depicted below. The curriculum contour is more expansive and invitational to exploration. There is not an assumption that we all come into the map at the same place or that we all explore the same parts of the map. It also suggests there is value in exploring different parts of the map and becoming experts in our part of the map. There is an invitation to share our "corner" of the map with others, and to meander across the map, varying according to interests, abilities, future expectations, and experiences, also supporting participation in ambiguous and transformational contexts.

Figure 3.3 Learning Terrains – Content Maps Versus Curriculum Contours

Traditional Content Map

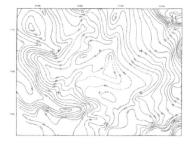

	Learning Outcomes				
Course Activities	Demonstrate	Analyze	Develop	Illustrate	Exhibit
A1					
A2					
A3					
A4					
A5					
A6					

Exploring Learning Contours

Another invitational possibility of a terrain view of the curriculum is for the learner to plant seeds and leave trails for future explorations and growth. Learning terrains or contours better accommodate pervasive, connected learning in information rich and technology infused environments while also laying the groundwork for lifelong and future learning. Futures learning, in particular, needs to be explored for understanding the kinds of skills, dispositions, and competencies we may need for surviving in our future; in a world that is currently in transition to one that will be transformed and transformational. The next chapter explores these futuring skills and understandings by exploring our relationship with the future.

Notes

Figure 3.3 Learning Terrains – Content Maps Versus Curriculum Contours. https://socratic.org/questions/how-do-contour-lines-show-hills-and-depressions. The image is released free of copyrights under Creative Commons CC0. You may download, modify, distribute, and use them royalty free for anything you like, even in commercial applications. Attribution is not required.

Chapter 4

Building Relationships With The Future

The 21st century is a pivotal turning point in human history. Just as the 13th-15th centuries marked fundamental changes in individual and social systems accompanied by political, scientific, religious, artistic, and technological innovations, the 20th and 21st centuries find us at the apex and end of an industrial-based economy with a focus on individuality and accomplishment, at the precipice of electronic and information revolutions that impose upon us the need to rethink core values and underlying myths about our purpose and place in this world. The Reformation and the Renaissance ushered in new ways of thinking, being, and valuing. The 21st century marks the beginning of this next epoch of humankind, marking a turning point begun in the 20th century with rapid technological advances and our ability to destroy the world and all life on it. Echoing ideas presented in Smyre and Richardson's *Preparing for a World That Doesn't Exist – Yet (2016)* the following are transformational challenges and guideposts:

- **Hyper-connectivity** signifies the need for a shift in our understanding of the single individual facing worlds' challenges to *connected individuality* where people, ideas, and processes are intricately linked and dynamically in relationship with one another. Environmental control and dominance need to give way to a goal for sustainable ecosystems where balance and harmony support evolution and adaptation as change from the individual perspective accommodates universal social and environmental nurturance.

- **Synergistic connections** communicates the expectation that survival of the fittest as the driving force for success needs to be replaced with *collaborative and synergistic connections* at deeper and deeper levels of involvement and meaning.

- **New metrics of success** at the social/economic level are based on the assumption of unending growth. This emphasis needs to be replaced by an economy that supports innovation and new wealth creation while challenging the existing pyramid structure of economic success with a very few at the top. New metrics of economic and societal success need to be accommodated in meaningful ways that cannot be manipulated or appropriated. New measures of societal and economic health need to be explored, as seen in New Zealand where the Gross National Product (GNP) was replaced by a happiness index as a measure of societal success.

- **Fearlessly engaging uncertainty** challenges the quest for certainty and dominance of ways of knowing that alienate and diminish huge portions of the population. By fearlessly engaging uncertainty we become empowered to create and invent the future, giving way to more inclusive, invitational, collaborative, and connected ways of knowing and being.

- **A new ethic** is required to deal with an emerging world view that matches the coming transformation of humans as social beings. This new ethic requires not only new tools and frameworks for thinking and learning, but new ways of defining and engaging a more fair and just way of being and decision making that supports sustainability and care for each other and our planet.

- **A new relationship with the future** is foundational to these new ways of thinking, being and acting ethically.

A New Relationship With The Future

To explore our relationship with the future to support changes in how we relate to the future and in anticipation of transformational times, it might be useful to first disrupt or reconsider standard conceptions of time.

Linear Time

Time, when perceived as linear moments marked by the passing of experiences or events, matches the way we think about time as defined in middle and high school mathematics which became the dominant way of thinking about time in Western civilization since the 16th century. Draw a horizontal line on paper. Draw another vertical line perpendicular to the horizontal timeline and you have the Cartesian plane developed by René Descartes in the 17th century. This way of looking at time is extremely valuable from a mathematical perspective. The Cartesian plane afforded scientists and mathematicians the means for understanding the relationships among motion and change captured by algebraic formulas. Seeing the repeating patterns of the sine or cosine curves provided insights into more complicated repeating patterns of heart rhythms and brain scans. Understanding geometric growth patterns of viruses gave us new ways to understand the spread of disease.

At the intersection of time as the horizontal axis and motion or growth as measured by the vertical access, is the zero point. The beginning. The "now." This nice, linear view of time separates the timeline into past, present and future. The past is what happens to the left of zero. The future is what happens to the right of zero. We use relationships from the past to make predictions about future relationships, as we learned in high school algebra to interpolate curves and look for repeating patterns.

We need a richer view of time to develop a more dynamic relationship with both the future AND the past. Think about this moment. Right now. Got it? It will never happen again. What about now? Got it? It's gone. It is now in the past. This "now" is now past. What about now. Nope, it's gone, too. Wait, how can there be meaning in these fleeting moments of now?

Futurists use a futures cone to consider possible, plausible, and desirable futures. I suggest we need an expanded notion of now that accommodates an expanded view of the present and past as well as an expanded view of the future and disrupts the moment-by-moment unfolding of linear time.

The Expanded Now

Craig Cunningham (2016) described John Dewey's ideas about experience as more dimensional and based not in fleeting moments of passing time but in situations or events, echoing how Whitehead (1929) defined fundamental existence as "drops of experience." Consider picking up a glove and smelling it. All of a sudden, at this present moment, you remember an event that occurred years ago. The smell reminds you of your grandmother. Maybe it is even your grandmother's glove. That experience you had and your conscious memory of it take you back to a time where you reconstruct the experience. You were in church, sitting with the grownups for the first time. Your grandmother held your hand with one gloved hand while the other cradled your shoulders. For many years in between, you never thought about this experience. But now, you reconstruct it, you remember it, and you reconnect with your past. This expanded "now" moment brings to conscious awareness a past situation and your interpretation of it. After remembering this past situation or life-event, maybe you put the glove away, and it fades into your past and unconscious awareness, again, but at least for these few moments, you remembered this wonderful experience.

Figure 4.1 Dewey's Event Epistemology and Memories of the Past

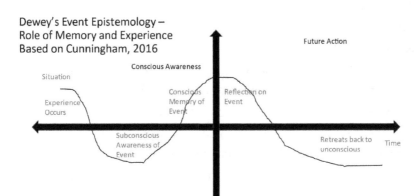

This view of time, while incorporating the richness of experience, still perceives time and events in our lives as linear unfoldings. It focuses on cognitive consciousness as events are experienced or as memories of events are experienced. What is needed is an expanded notion of time that incorporates a more comprehensive view of the event-experience relationship as time, itself, fluidly is experienced and re-experienced. This is the idea of the "expanded now."

An "expanded now" elicits mind, heart and gut responses to past and future events. It also suggests our current conscious awareness of an event or situation is still our constructed interpretation of that event.

As the diagram below suggests, perhaps when you picked up the glove a few moments ago, you responded to the smell, your gut way of knowing, and your heart-knowing provided a feeling of joy or happiness, in addition to your cognitive way of knowing by remembering the past event. This moment when you picked up the glove and smelled it was a disequilibriating event that prompted your mind, heart and gut responses. Maybe we are not even aware of our heart and gut ways of knowing but they contribute to the richness of our memories and experiences. The dotted line in the diagram below from our current moment of conscious awareness of the past situation or event is our reconstructed memory. Maybe how we remembered it, however, wasn't how it happened at all. What we are remembering isn't the event, but our construction of the event. If your grandmother were still alive, in the example with the glove, you could hear her side of what happened. Maybe what she would say is that you were squirming and making noise and not sitting still and that your mother was getting madder and madder by the minute. So, she grabbed you and basically forced you to sit still. What you interpreted as a loving embrace was her effort to keep you still. **The expanded now not only doesn't assume our memories of the past are accurate, but also invites these larger ways of thinking about a past event to be included as we interpret our past.**

Figure 4.2 Expanded Now Experiences

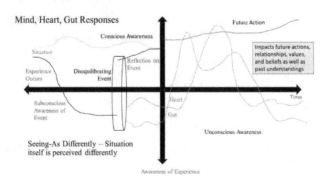

The Expanded Now resulting from this disequilibriating event allows us to expand our understanding of the past through the reconstructive process. By opening up the idea that events are not "objectively" written in the past, we can develop a deeper understanding of the past as we prepare for the future. For example, during the Black Lives Matter protests of the 2020s, many Whites, especially in the United States, were challenged to rethink our society's racist past. The stories we were told about statues to confederate generals, especially in the South, were unraveled as we now looked at the event of their construction in the early 20th century, in many cases sponsored by associations with ties to White Supremacy, as an act of defiance by Southern Whites who wanted to subliminally communicate to minorities that they better behave. Our re-examining the past through a different lens allows for what Wittgenstein (1953) described as "seeing-as differently." Many cognitive therapies, for example Buddhist psychology, also invite a look to the past and the future with "soft-eyes." **Seeing with soft eyes shifts focus from the direct event to the peripheral events surrounding the event.** It is only through seeing-as differently, according to Wittgenstein, that we can have fundamental, transformative change.

An understanding of the Expanded Now and the relationship with our reconstructed and expanded views of the past are necessary for engaging and creating possible, plausible and desirable futures, especially during times of transformational change.

Developing a Relationship with the Future

The Adaptive Futures Cone (below) shows an expanded now as it interacts with both the past and future. The expanded now allows us to get beyond our own memories or even beyond critical consciousness that challenges individual or collective past memories, experiences and histories, to see-as differently. By expanding our views of the past, we are able to expand possibilities for the future.

As the Adaptive Futures Cone represents, in a narrow sense, we can work towards probable or preferred futures, based on unquestioned views of the present. These probable or preferred futures are important for everyday survival. Do I carry my umbrella or not? What are the things I need to do to best prepare for the next economic downturn (assuming the economy of the future has the same structure as the current economy)? What strategy shall I use in this chess match? How much time should I leave for homework, and can I fit in dinner with friends?

Riel Miller (2018) calls these kinds of relationship with the future predictive and optimizing and are part of foresight that guides much of everyday action and decision making. We can use models to predict the future, assuming weather patterns and prototypes that have worked in the past continue to be relevant or the rules of the game have not changed. We can optimize our choices by balancing risk and managing time to ensure the best possible outcomes.

But how do we support relationships with the future during times of rapid change or times of social transformation when the past may not serve us well as viable patterns for the future? How do we create the kinds of futures we want to support new ways of thinking and interacting? How do we accommodate shifts in ethical expectations, values and understandings? Answers to these questions will become important as we consider the future of learning during transformational times.

There are specific futuring tools that can facilitate an Expanded Now perspective to support futures learning. These tools can facilitate going beyond status quo thinking about the future to create new possibilities that will be more appropriate and vitally important in the coming era of human existence.

Figure 4.3 Adapted Futures Cone

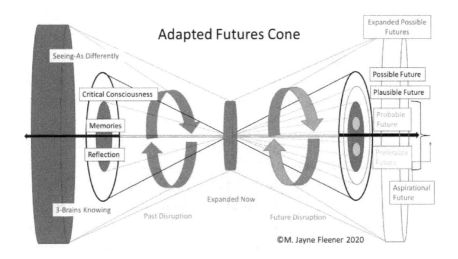

Adaptive Futures Learning

Sohail Inayatullah (2008) lists six basic questions to ask about the future.

1. What do you think the future will be like?

2. Which future are you afraid of?

3. What are the hidden assumptions of your predicted future?

4. What are some alternatives to your predicted or feared future?

5. What is your preferred future?

6. How might you make your preferred future occur?

These questions are especially important to explore when the emergent future is based on ideas and methods that do not currently exist and the preferred future challenges the basic assumptions of a predicted future based on existing knowledge.

As each of these questions is explored, it is important, especially during transformational periods, to think deeply about the past, present and future, and these questions can help us do that. From a perspective of the Expanded Now, these questions allow us to understand in the present, as these questions are explored, the seeds of future possibilities and rethink the past in ways that deepen our insights. And because the unexamined past cannot provide useful guidance for the uncertain future, a deeper look at the past through an "Extended Now" perspective is especially important for seeing with new eyes in order to expose hidden assumptions and create new possibilities.

In this section, we will build on the challenges inherent in the myths of the past discussed in Chapter 3 to explore expanded ways of thinking about the future of learning. Below is an example of how the Extended Now can provide ways of rethinking future action by remembering our own mistakes or exposing past hidden assumptions as educators. All educators, in hindsight, remember moments when they taught something, only to discover years later that what they taught was wrong. Sometimes the errors are because of new discoveries. And sometimes these errors are because we made assumptions or had world views that went unchallenged.

Personal Reflection of Unexamined Assumptions

As a classroom teacher, we all have moments, just as parents, where we have answered a question and later regretted our answer, recognizing the inadequacy of our answer at the time and in retrospect as situations have evolved. There are two questions, in particular, that I (Jayne) remember being asked when

I taught computer programming in the 1980s whose answers I now recognize as limited, limiting, and wrong. And both answers, I should have anticipated at the time and certainly recognize now as having been short-sighted.

The first question had to do with what kinds of problems computers could solve. The computer literacy literature in the early 1980s emphasized that computers could only solve problems they were programmed to solve and that they could not solve really hard, complex, "wicked" problems. The assumption, at the time, was that only the human mind was capable of addressing the complexity of these kinds of problems and inventing new ways to address them. When students asked why computers could not solve war or why we had to give a computer specific instructions using a special computer language code, I did not challenge the curriculum or question why we couldn't just "talk" instructions to a computer. (At this very time in the early 1980s, Steven Jobs was questioning these assumptions and inventing new ways of interacting with technology that ultimately lead to our ability to ask Sirius *Who won the LSU game last night?*)

The other question I was asked was whether personal information was secure when saved on computers. The question came up in the context of medical records being stored by computers. At the time, in the early 1980s, this issue was just beginning to be explored. Of course, your data would be secure, I answered. At the time, there was no internet as we know it today and we already had encryption software, so of course the answer was yes – information and data were secure. People who worried were being anti-progressive!

What I failed to do at the time, even in a quickly changing field like computer science, **was to recognize and explore the full potential of the changes yet to come with computer technology.** I should have anticipated the internet since the schools where I taught actually had access to the Triangle University

Computing Consortium (TUCC) through a phone modem device the size of a desk. The modem allowed my high schools to connect through TUCC to the major research universities in the Research Triangle area of North Carolina. I knew computer security was going to be an issue and even discussed the possible vulnerability of computer billing systems for nefarious employees to skim a penny off everyone's electric bill to become rich with automatic customer billing fraud. And I had anticipated my students' early efforts to hack into the university computing systems to see if they had been admitted by developing policies about their access.

Weak Signals

In retrospect, there were hints of things to come that when the past is reconsidered, we can recognize from our future vantage point. These hints to the future have been referred to as **weak signals**. In my expanded now, I can go back and see in my 1980s world how the Internet was being born and how the hard-wired connections required at the time were just the beginning of hyper-connected computers, virtual networks, and evolving computing power. Other weak signals were the rapid changes in technology. I began teaching computer science on "micro" and "mini" computers, some that had only 4K of memory and no way of storing data. Even my first MacIntosh computer in 1984 did not have an internal disk drive, yet in a period of five years we transitioned very quickly from a relatively transparent black box of computing power to complex, internal operations and interconnective systems that were becoming more and more powerful, smaller, less transparent/accessible and cheaper by the year.

Missed Opportunity

Had I engaged the six questions above, inviting my students

to explore these ideas as well, we may have anticipated the emerging fields and careers of computer data security, Big Data systems analytics, applications architecture, web development, computer hardware and software engineering, medical and computer ethics, systems design, and information sciences. We could have anticipated the impact of miniaturization on medical devices and explored the ethics of implants, CRISPR, and other technology-enabled advances.

Futurists use a variety of futuring tools with clients to facilitate their exploration of possible and preferrable futures. With the advent of the concepts of connectivity and emergence, a number of futurists have come to realize that one is not able to predict specific outcomes in a constantly transforming society and economy, but is able to look for connections among emerging new ideas that will provide a "futures context" very different from the past. Formal and informal learning engagements should similarly develop these skills for anticipating and shaping the expanded views of the future. A few of these tools will be described below to facilitate the development of approaches to the future of learning that suggest radical transformation of institutional, formal learning environments that parallel the advances we have seen in informal and nonformal learning approaches.

Futuring Techniques

Futures Wheel

The **Futures Wheel** (Bishop & Hines, 2016) is perhaps the most basic place to begin an exploration to address possible futures. Like the spokes of an ever-expanding wheel, the Futures Wheel explores societal, technological, environmental, economic, political, and artistic dimensions of a problem as possible futures are explored. These dimensions are given acronyms like STEEPA to ensure a layered analysis across multiple facets of human invention and activity. When used in parallel with an expanded futures perspective that embraces emergent futures' possibilities and desires, the futures wheel can support development of and facilitate conversations about desirable futures and worlds that do not yet exist. The futures wheel can further support adaptive planning that accommodates shifting contexts, unpredictable novelty, interconnected and accelerating contexts, and emergent connections characteristic of transformational times.

For example, suppose we take the problem of the long-term impact of COVID-19. A futures wheel might identify initial changes in social and behavioral impacts associated with hand washing, social distancing, and self-isolation. Many states publicized acronyms like "the Three W's – Wear a mask, Wait six-feet apart, Wash your hands." Other immediate social responses included closing large-venue facilities, restaurants, churches and schools.

Stay-at-home mandates as an early response to the COVID-19 pandemic impacted social as well as economic or business relationships, resulted in loss of jobs and near-collapse of certain economies. Technological impacts included the need for technological solutions to support tele-work, conferencing, and virtual meetings in many business sectors. From an environmental perspective, closing public facilities and workplaces had an unintended positive environmental impact on pollution and gas consumption while having severe negative impacts on the economy and small businesses. From an artistic or cultural perspective, people staying at home developed new interests and talents such as cooking, playing a musical instrument and developing new hobbies. By exploring impacts from the STEEPA perspectives, a wider array of understandings and possibilities about the future can be explored.

Going further out in the futures wheel, second and third order impacts provide additional guidance and reveal possible weak signals about the future. For example, as we practiced the Three-W's, public spaces placed new barriers and notices to ensure the safety of workers and patrons including plastic shields at registers and six-foot markers on the floor. Businesses developed new work-at-home policies and work-surveillance and accountability measures. Responses to loss of work and income required food distribution strategies and policies to prevent eviction of individuals from their homes who were forced out of jobs and could not pay their rent. These challenges were also met by individuals and civic organizations taking up the slack where local, state and federal responses were inadequate. Churches developed online religious services and vaccine development and approval were fast-tracked.

We can use the Futures Wheel to continue to analyze how we responded across the first three or four levels of response then start to examine the possible, probable and desirable futures of the impact of the COVID-19 virus as we extend our layers into the future. We may start to debate whether we go back to "normal," pre-pandemic activities or how and whether there are fundamental changes across the STEEPA categories necessary to accommodate the New Normal. For example, while some have experienced "Zoom fatigue" with too many virtual meetings, it is likely that virtual meetings will become a part of the future landscape of business, education, and personal connections. This may have major impact on facilities and physical workspace requirements for companies. Wearing masks in public may become a routine activity, and long-term economic impacts may enable new understandings and expectations for social services, charitable activities, and values for protecting the most vulnerable in society.

The sample Futures Wheel below, while likely impossible to read, gives a visual sense of how the layers get played out.

While often used only to look at future possibilities, with our Expanded Now perspective, the first several layers of the wheel include both past and present STEEPA understandings while the outer bands start to envision and articulate the kinds of futures we may want, and expose the possible futures we most fear.

Figure 4.4 Futures Wheel for COVID-19

Futures Wheel Exploring Possible and Desirable Impacts of COVID-19

The Futures Wheel can be a beginning place to address the first five questions about the future presented above. Additional strategies can be used to explore the sixth question: How might you make your preferred future occur? The next strategy we will explore is the Integral Futures matrix. Additional futures approaches are important to address the "unknown unknowns" as pronounced by former US Secretary of Defense, Donald Rumsfeld, that become so important in futures learning engagements.

Futures Triangle

The Futures Triangle is another tool described by Inayatullah (2008) that helps explore historical influences and present contexts to consider possible and plausible futures. As the Expanded Futures Cone (see figure 4.3) reveals, disrupting linear time requires both a re-examination of possible futures but a reconsideration of the past.

As the six questions about the future are explored, the Futures Triangle is especially helpful for exploring what the future may be like and exposing what you may be afraid of in the future. It also begins to expose the hidden assumptions of predicted futures and opens spaces for discussing alternatives to predicted futures.

Figure 4.5 Futures Triangle

Futures Triangle

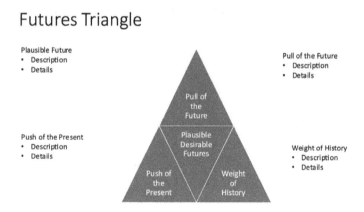

Students using the Futures Triangle find the Push of the Present and the Weight of History particularly difficult to distinguish. Futurists using the Futures Triangle strategy also find a lack of understanding about the Weight of History can greatly diminish the outcomes and possibilities explored as possible, plausible and desirable futures.

The Futures Triangle is especially useful when developing different scenarios for the future. A valuable strategy for exploring possible, plausible, and desirable futures combines Schwartz's Four Scenarios method with the Futures Triangle to develop Best Case, Worst Case, Outlier, and Business-as-Usual scenarios (Dator, 2017).

Integral Futures Matrix

Ken Wilber (Slaughter, 2020) first described the Integral Futures Model to facilitate decision making strategies to implement change initiatives for creating preferred futures. The basis for this model is the idea that our interactions, understandings, and behaviors are multi-dimensional. He describes the inner-outer dimension as well as the individual-social dimension that impact potential futures, as seen in the quadrant map and 2x2 matrix below.

Figure 4.6 Integral Futures Matrix

Integral Futures Matrix and Four Quadrant Mapping

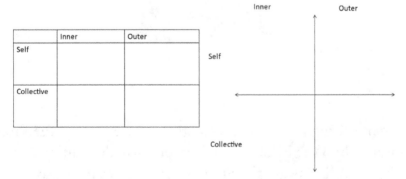

The upper left quadrant of the IF matrix explores identity and meaning for individuals. Because the inner world of our individual understandings is difficult to determine and requires a degree of interpretation and reflection, developing strategies for reflective practice and identity development become important for futures work. The Expanded Now reflection on past experiences, feelings, memories, and histories become a part of the Inner-Self exploration. And especially because, as we have already explored with the myths of the modern era in Chapter 3, our identities have been wrapped up in our work and social status, we need to think about future possibilities that also challenge **how we individually will derive meaning and a sense of self in the future**.

The bottom left quadrant of the IF map deepens this exploration of identity and meaning. When working with groups, this is often the hardest quadrant to explore because so many societal expectations and meanings have gone unexamined. One way to explore the inner-collective space is to explore the language we use. Language and culture are very much a part of the collective perspective of who we are and how we pursue meaning in life. Even the language we use to describe work or communicate values represent cultural worldviews. The language of either-or logic with an implied right way to do things is communicated at the collective level and constrains our ability to think about possibilities for the future. As Wittgenstein described, to have a change in aspect, a fundamental change in how we think, we need to change our language. This needs to occur at both individual and collective levels. It is important when addressing the tacit understandings and expectations of a society by examining the language we use and the meanings we share, we may need to be willing to and be required to replace these meaning structures and world views implicit in our shared cultures. We saw this with the Feminist movement of the 1970s as "history" was exposed as "His-Story" and "Herstory" was used. Even then, however, we did not escape the dualistic way of thinking about our past. Especially during transformational times, as we explore possible futures, we need to be willing to expose and go beyond existing mores. As we have seen with the modern assumptions about our culture, myths and the language of progress, either-or logic, and hierarchies are prevalent in the language we use but maladaptive for the era to which we are about to transition. In the internal-collective quadrant that defines a society's culture, we need to **reexamine our social metaphors, myths, and language to create new understandings of who we are and where we are going as a society**.

The right side of the IF framework is more visible and measurable. The upper right quadrant examines explicit behaviors and capacities of individuals. When we explore the potential, possible and preferred futures, here is where **we describe what life looks like for individuals**, the skills they have, and the jobs they occupy. This is the area where most of education focuses with preparing individuals to participate in their world through the work they do and their individual accomplishments. During the modern era, there is the underlying myth that individual autonomy and accomplishment drive individuals and are measured by how much education they have, how much they can purchase, the houses they live in, and the wealth they have acquired. Measures of knowing are used in the individual exterior domain, feeding back to individual feelings and beliefs about intelligence. **In the current transitional times, we need to think about future ways of being in a world where work and jobs do not define success and cannot even be anticipated.** In the world of the future, as we explore the possibilities, we need to disrupt these myths of consumerism and individual wealth in favor of **more sustainable metrics of accomplishments that support "connected individuality" and adaptive capabilities**.

Finally, the bottom right of the IF framework describes what the physical and social world looks like. When organizations think about the future, they often think in terms of competitive market share, number of customers, and profit. We often measure our self-worth, in the first quadrant, by outcomes we can define and compare with measures in the fourth quadrant. How well do we compete? What are the measures of social success that provide evidence of our worth? **The expected and accepted outcomes of a society focused on competition and accountability during the modern era may be poor markers for rethinking a different kind of emergent social and economic success we will need in the future.**

As we use the IF model to explore possible and desirable futures when outcomes can be identified, as well as apply the principles of "emergent connectivism" when "black swans[1]" appear unexpectedly, we need to keep in mind the myths about learning we defined earlier that have evolved in the modern era and disrupt these ways of thinking and being to create new ways of thinking about the future. These myths are presented below in the quadrants where they are most relevant. There is, however, overlap with some unmeasurable, individual and social interior perspectives being defined and measured by external metrics. As we explore the kinds of futures we want to create and the kind of learning we need once we have an understanding of transformational creativity based on connecting newly emergent ideas that cannot be predicted, we also need to expose and address these underlying myths.

---

1   Black Swans are unexpected and unpredictable events

Figure 4.7 Example of IF Approach to Overcoming Myths & Addressing Transformational Challenges

Integral Futures Approach to Overcoming Myths and Addressing Transformational Challenges

	Inner	Outer
Self	New meanings of self in the future Adaptive capabilities	Redefine what life looks like for individuals Collective individuality
Collective	Re-examine social metaphors, myths and language to understand where we are going as a society	Redefine social success

	Inner	Outer
Self	Myths of Individual autonomy, knowledge acquisition & accomplishment	Myths of Consumerism, and individual wealth
Collective	Myths of progress, either-or logic, and hierarchies	Myths of Competition, SWOT, Outcomes and Accountability

> Addressing Transformational Challenges

> Replacing these myths

As IF strategies broaden our view of possible and desirable futures, it is clear how failure to address the underlying myths and challenges of the modern era may not open the possibilities we need to think about the future during transformational times. A final strategy to be explored, defined by Inayatullah (2008), is Causal Layered Analysis and will be described below.

Causal Layered Analysis (CLA)

The Futures Wheel and Integral Futures Framework are useful tools for exploring possible futures within the framework of existing assumptions and with the possibility of extending these frameworks to accommodate "unknown unknowns." While we have built in strategies for the Extended Now and exposure of underlying myths and frameworks within these strategies, the CLA approach is a deliberate approach to "deepening the future" (Inayatullah, 2008) with specific attention to problema-

tizing these underlying myths and metaphors that may perpetuate problems beyond immediate fixes. It is a process that can
be used with the other two tools to ensure our ideas about the
future go beyond replicating status quo and address the needs
of our future, transformed society.

Figure 4.8 Causal Layered Analysis

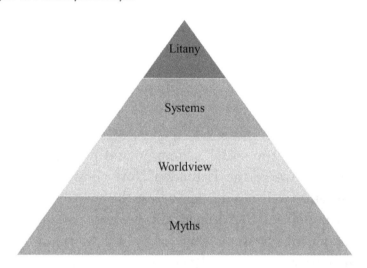

The above image has two visual metaphors to distinguish this
process as a "deepening" futures process. Like the "tip of an
iceberg," the Litany and Systems levels of analysis are fairly
transparent as data is collected and analyzed across social systems categories. The field of Foresight often focuses on Litany
and Systems analyses to make predictions and reveal patterns
of influence to facilitate future action. These layers of the CLA
are very useful during times of stability but in times of great
uncertainty, the layers "below the surface" expose underlying
myths and metaphors that could impact fundamental change
during transformational times. Like the root-system of a tree
or below-the-surface of an iceberg, these underlying myths
and metaphors and subsequent new myths and metaphors are
expansive and far reaching.

The first step of the CLA approach is called **"Litany"** and supports an initial exploration of a problem at hand. During the Litany phase of the CLA, we look at our day-to-day understandings of how things are and how they should be. Like the religious litany at a church service, strategies at this stage tend to be routine. For example, suppose we were addressing the problem of food insecurity during the pandemic. At the Litany stage, we would explore where there are the greatest needs and develop a strategy for food distribution. The solution, at the Litany stage addresses the immediate need, in this case, the distribution of food. How things are: there are people who don't have enough food. How things should be: no one should go hungry. Solution: distribute food to those who need it. What it does not do is prepare for a world that is constantly transforming (see the work of Ruben Nelson, 2010).

At the second stage of the CLA, we go deeper than the immediate problem to explore the social, economic and political causes of the problem. This is where the Extended Now allows for an historical re-examination as well as a deeper look at the current contexts. Direct causes and/or policies that impact the problem are explored at the **Going Deeper into Systems** stage of the CLA. So, in our example of food insecurity, at a deeper level, we may look at the challenge of students being out of school where they received free and reduced lunches and develop solutions that may include working with funding agencies that have supported the school lunch program to make resources available to children who are not in school due to the pandemic.

At the third stage of the CLA, we take a wider, cultural or world view of the problem. At the **Worldview** level or exploration, we explore the paradigms and perspectives that inform the reality of the problem we are exploring. This level also invites an Extended Now critical examination of the problem. So back to our example of food insecurity, we may recognize the over-representation of minorities and particular zip codes in the city that are most dramatically impacted by food insecurity. The long-standing challenges of red-lining that creates pockets of poverty within our community come to play in the solution to the problem. The immediate need of feeding the community exposes the deeper challenges of institutional and geographic racism, the lack of grocery stores and farmer's markets in the vicinity to provide fresh vegetables and fruit at reasonable prices, and the long-standing challenges of generational poverty, lack of job opportunities, and underemployment. A world-view based on slavery mentality creates long-standing policies and practices that make an underclass possible.

Finally, at the fourth stage of the CLA is an exploration of the underlying, unconscious stories and deep myths that are factors behind the problem. At the **mythical level**, an exploration such as the one we conducted at the beginning of this chapter on the myths of education exposes deeper challenges but also presents more sustainable options and opportunities to address the problem. Underlying the food insecurity challenge is the myth of rugged individualism and the idea that the people who are being challenged are somehow to blame because of their lack of success. It is easy for well-meaning citizens to perpetuate dependencies and inadvertently communicate perceptions of failure to those in need, creating a sense of shame and feelings of defeat among those we serve. This important fourth stage helps us identify and break out of the cycle of knee-jerk responses to problems to explore underlying myths or metaphors that contribute to the perpetuation of the problem.

Figure 4.9 CLA Example – Food Insecurity

Causal Layered Analysis – Food Insecurity Example

- **Litany** – Look at the situation and distribute food to those who need it.
- **Going Deeper in Systems** – Look at direct causes and policies that impact food insecurity such as students who are out of school during the pandemic where they usually receive free and reduced lunches.
- **Worldview** – A worldview based on slavery mentality creates long-standing policies and practices that reinforce a permanent underclass; strategies need to be examined for how this worldview may be disrupted.
- **Myths** – The myth of rugged individualism puts blame on those in need, creating feelings of shame, defeat and resentment; solutions need to overcome perpetuation of this myth and these dependencies.

These four futures strategies along with the Extended Now perspective are important for exploring how we anticipate and create learning needs and opportunities for learners in our next era of existence. The next chapter will explore learning needs for individuals as they navigate the rapid changes of a society in transition and explore the role of the learning ecosystem in preparing for and supporting a very different society of the future.

Notes

Figure 4.4 Futures Wheel for COVID-19.
Futures Wheel generated from template. https://online.visual-paradigm.com/diagrams/templates/futures-wheel/futures-wheel-template/

Chapter 5

Creating Futures Learning Ecosystems

The answers to the question about how we construct and coordinate learning systems in the future have to come from communities, influenced by and in coordination with the world community of our planet. A futures learning ecosystem will facilitate these conversations and transformations.

The future is not written, and this chapter is not about predicting the future. The goal of this chapter is to help people **think about how to support learning needs in the future and, at the same time, bring forth the future we need**. The assumption has been that we are, in fact, at the precipice of a new human era on this planet. The process of inventing new possibilities for the future includes exposing and changing our ideas about some deeply held beliefs that have served (many of) us well for over 500 years, developing new strategies for thinking, learning and doing that open up possibilities for deep changes to occur, and engaging as communities in opportunities to envision and enact a future that is going to be very different from the past. In exploring our ideas about futures learning ecosystems, we are creating and supporting the mindset for very different futures.

A guiding metaphor for this discussion comes from complex adaptive systems theory. A complex adaptive system is dynamic and open to change. Unleashing the potential of a complex adaptive system includes creating rich environments for supporting open, complex systems to emerge and thrive. The learning ecosystem is just one component of a rich environment that will contribute to a social system that has capacities to change, adapt, and grow as we transition to transformational times. The components of a Futures Learning Ecosystem will be described below.

Figure 5.1 Futures Learning Ecosystem

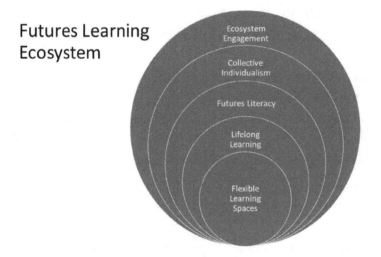

Flexible Learning Spaces

At the core of our futures learning ecosystem is the creation and support of flexible learning spaces. As we saw with the learning contours discussed in Chapter 3, rather than a set of competencies and skills mandated as prerequisites for future learning, flexibility includes **flexible curricula, methods, contexts, and learning relationships.**

During the COVID-19 pandemic, we have seen glimpses of a vision that suggests students do not need to spend five days a week, six hours a day in a formal school setting. Students from families of means especially combine **virtual, formal schooling with outdoor experiences, travel, arts and crafts, community service, exercise and healthcare, and other hobbies such as cooking and computer design**. These kinds of opportunities should be made available to all students as we also challenge a curriculum that for many students is tedious, at best, and meaningless in the worst case.

While some students have suffered during virtual learning, others have thrived. Some of the challenges of virtual learning, have been exacerbated by curriculum content that is distributed to all students with the same expectations for pacing and accomplishment. Complicated class schedules are posted on refrigerators with 30 – 60-minute time slots for different content lessons. The fragmented curriculum that separates content into disciplinary knowledge needs to be replaced with holistic approaches to learning that support **rich and meaningful learning opportunities** combining traditional content across many different disciplines and approaches. It is the emphasis on connecting emerging disparate ideas and factors not previously identified that is the basis for "transformational learning."

Personal Reflection

I (Jayne) used to work hard to come up with rich problems in mathematics classes that could be solved in many different ways. Sometimes, the most advanced students who had the most mathematics background had more trouble with these problems than the students who had more intuitive ways of solving them. This became really apparent when I would offer workshops for elementary through advanced upper high school mathematics teachers. While the advanced math teachers would try to solve problems using algebra or calculus or some obscure polar plane analysis, the elementary teachers would draw pictures and create charts to solve the problems. Neither solution approach was better than the other and we all learned something interesting by seeing the very different approaches. Just as I had seen in my computer programming classes, solving interesting problems and being encouraged to approach them in different ways made all the difference in their interest, engagement and learning. The core learning structures needed could be learned, as needed. Seeing the different approaches and heuristic styles and making connections across different approaches was more valuable than getting the right answer.

Educational Contours

Educational contours as a way to understand **curricular relationships** invites rich exploration of various landscapes. Not everyone needs to be in the same learning landscape to develop core understandings and shared meanings. Some prefer ocean landscapes. Other the mountains. Some cold climates. These environmental landscape preferences are analogous to learning landscapes. For example, volunteering in a community soup kitchen can provide rich opportunities for a variety of learning skills and understandings while supporting a child's civic participation passions.

As with many other aspects of our transformational world, a **both-and understanding supports flexible learning spaces** where learning skills AND learning applications are encouraged through interest-driven learning engagements where present context and an emerging "futures context" are evolved in parallel. Not everyone needs to have the same approaches or academic understandings—they don't anyhow!

What makes these experiences learning engagements is highly dependent on the skill of a **master facilitator** or **mas-**

ter capacity builder and lover of content understandings and disciplinary connections. Master facilitators can be found in formal as well as informal educational settings. We see this as caring parents develop their children's skills, interests and talents by creating experiences and opportunities for them. We will explore master capacity building more from the perspective of leadership skills and community capacity building, but these same skills can be utilized in the classroom and in learning contexts.

We need to expand our understandings of the learning relationships we expect, especially in formal settings. In formal education, the primary learning relationship is between the student and the teacher. Even in classrooms with skilled teachers who understand how to orchestrate learning symphonies with blended skills and harmonious activities among student peers, the teacher-student relationship is the single most important relationship in classrooms. And, ultimately, the teacher today assigns grades to student work as an estimation of their learning against some pre-defined scale or metric. There is still the need for skilled teachers who can find the educative opportunities within various activities and experiences, but the driver of learning needs to shift from the teacher-as-chauffeur to **student-as-navigator**. This shift also supports the shift away from formal education to support lifelong, informal and nonformal learning.

For some, the student-as-navigator metaphor is not new. For the cynical few who remember the open curriculum of the 1960s with distain, this may sound like a reappropriation of Dewey's progressive education with its rejection of adult-imposed understandings and disciplinary organization force-fed to all students as scope and sequenced curricula. As prescient as these ideas were at the time, they take on new meanings as we prepare to transition to transformational times where change is so pervasive that we cannot be expected to learn everything.

Our goals for formal education, in support of developing skills for nonformal and informal learning, need to remain focused on lifelong learning among connected individuals supported by flexible learning environments in an age of constant change, new knowledge and technology, and disruptive social, economic and environmental transformations.

As we saw in informal and nonformal education, grades, assessments and standard measures are not important in lifelong learning outcomes. We have discussed the myths of assessment, accountability, learning units and completion. If formal education needs some form of accountability metrics, a **Blockchain education approach** could incorporate learning outcomes as a lifelong accounting of educative experiences. The value of a blockchain approach is that, unlike our current system of grading and credentialing, no one owns the blockchain. Each individual owns their own node which can be made available to anyone permitted by the individual owner. This is consistent with the need to understand learning from an "emergent ecosystem" point of view. If an employer is looking to hire someone with experiences in computer game design, a student could share parts of their blockchain node that conveys relevant experiences, products, outcomes, and engagements. The blockchain credentialling of educational accomplishment emerges and evolves throughout our lifetime, supporting lifelong learning.

Lifelong Learning

One of the current challenges or myths about education is that once we graduate, we feel our learning is over. We are done. We don't need to learn any more. And for many, the desire to learn, especially in formal settings, has been extinguished. The emphasis on academic credentials perpetuates this myth that the most important learning is captured by the completion of specific credentials. Blockchain educational outcomes supports a more fluid understanding of learning as an on-going, unending, continuous process that can follow us throughout our lifetime. The unfolding of these educative experiences is also important to the futures learning ecosystem during transformational times.

A part of lifelong learning is also developing our intuitions, insights, passions and interests, supporting **heart and gut learning** as well as cognitive-mind learning. Likewise, lifelong learning supports continuous **learning, uplearning and unlearning**—important processes in continuous, harmonious learning landscapes. Uplearning and unlearning provides opportunities for the **connective learner** continuously to make sense of, reflect on, and evaluate new approaches to learning that are consistent with an emerging age that will be increasingly fast-paced, interconnected, interdependent and complex. Developing this reflective practice deepens learning, builds in an Expanded Now and Emergent Futures parallel perspective for learning, and provides opportunities for transcendent experiences and explorations of the ethical consequences of what we learn.

During transformational times, long-range planning, goals and visions are replaced with seeing with "soft eyes" in an environment that is constantly changing. As we saw with the Extended Now, seeing-as differently is a key strategy for making sense of our experiences to facilitate deep change and navigate uncertainty. Seeing-as differently includes blurring what we think we know, looking beyond accepted ways of knowing, and seeing with soft eyes to allow our peripheral vision to provide new insights and different connections that transform how we approach a constantly changing future. Rather than thinking about what we want to be doing in 10 years, we need to be able to adapt to change and embrace opportunities as they occur, adapting to change with an ever-present eye to the unknown unknowns. We need learning-to-learn strategies that include seeing with soft eyes strategies to maintain an openness to possibilities.

Another component of lifelong learning is developing and **exploring intuitions** about learning needs—also a part of gut and heart learning. Teachers need to help students learn to listen to their intuitions about their own learning needs and interests and design learning opportunities that support lifelong learning that will sustain students' interests, passions and learning needs throughout their lifetimes. Developing intuitions about learning needs is an important skill to sustain lifelong learning.

We have explored **pervasive learning** in Chapter 3 as it relates to ubiquitous technology and informal and nonformal learning. As described previously, pervasive learning is a good model for how formal education needs to change, as well. The opportunities to pursue tangents, follow whims, and learn skills as needed should drive learning even during formal education.

Developing and supporting curiosity is driven by learning how to **ask creative questions. Seeding new ideas** comes from asking great questions and helping students make connections across diverse ideas, people, processes and outcomes. Knowing "where" to look becomes more important than a robotic knowing "what." Because the "what's" of the future are changing, having ready answers is not nearly as valuable as knowing the right questions, a key focus of this time of historical transformation.

Supporting lifelong learning is a futures literacy skill with its emphasis on creativity, emergence, and ways of knowing that includes intuition, insight, imagination, innovation, inspiration, passion, as well as traditional ways of knowing and doing. Futures literacy as an important part of the Futures Learning Ecosystem will be explored below.

Futures Literacy

Our relationship with the future goes beyond forecasting and foresight. Knowing whether to carry an umbrella in case of rain or how to develop a strategy to win at chess are useful for known systems with predictable rules and outcomes. But in our transformational world, other futures skills take on new importance.

These futures skills include abilities to **create, invent, inspire and inform**. These skills are part of what has previously been described in chapter 1 as Mindflex. As discussed previously, there are futuring skills and techniques that can be learned, but more importantly, there is an approach to learning that becomes part of the futures learning ecosystem. This approach to learning includes a willingness to question underlying assumptions and dig deeply into underlying myths, metaphors, and systems that prevent change. In order for the futures learning ecosystem to support the complex adaptive system of a society in transformational times, the openness to challenging status quo must be supported. While we have touted critical thinking as an important part of the current formal education ecosystem, we have done so in an environment that does not support futures critical thinking, innovation, and questioning of status quo. Futures literacy as a core component of the futures learning ecosystem truly supports critical, disruptive thinking as important for individual as well as social systems learning.

Several initiatives sponsored by UNESCO (United Nations Educational, Scientific and Cultural Organization) include Futures Literacy Labs as convenings for key stakeholders to create, invent, and inspire future activities in their communities. Futures literacy, as a component of the futures learning ecosystem, supports connective individualism, replacing the myths of individual autonomy, success, progress and competition in favor of collaborative and collective impact.

Connective Individualism

We tend to think of learning as something we do individually, but part of the futures learning ecosystem is the role we play in co-creating future possibilities during times of rapid change. We have discussed the myth of the rugged individual as maladaptive for the coming transformational times. Replacing this myth of the rugged individual who can pull themselves up by their bootstraps is the idea of connective individualism. This is an "and/both" understanding of the importance of individual articulation of self and a recognition of our interconnectedness and need to participate in efforts for the greater good. Collective individualism goes beyond the idea that a rising tide of one raises all boats, to considerations of the implications of interrelationships for **synergizing collective efforts to the benefit of all** as a social good.

As part of the sustaining ecosystem of a society during transformational times, the learning ecosystem that develops and supports collective individualism encourages diverse understandings and connections across race, ethnicity, social status, sexual orientation, family constitution, and history. **Diversity is important** for the sustenance of a rich ecosystem and is to be celebrated and used to synergize creativity and impact for more sustainable, fair, caring and supportive social systems. What Smyre and Richardson (2016) refer to as futures-generative dialogue is supported by learning environments that include diverse individuals and perspectives and nurture collective individualism and co-creation of possible futures.

Finally, the futures learning ecosystem supports engagements that facilitate and support social transformation. Ecosystem engagement is the final layer of the futures learning ecosystem that creates and encourages a dynamic relationship with the social-world environment.

Ecosystem Engagement

An important function of education during the modern era was for workforce development. Education was the training ground for basic skills and dispositions so future employees could matriculate from school environments to work environments. But as workplaces have become more complex and are rapidly changing, a common complaint by many companies is that workers are not prepared for their complex work environments. Business and industry spend a great deal of money on retraining and other supports for new employees. The misalignment between formal education and the workplace is a consequence of a "linear learning" process designed in a different time for different purposes. As the new futures learning ecosystem evolves, across layers of flexible learning spaces, lifelong learning expectations, futures literacy, and connective individualism, future citizens of the world will be better enabled and have the desires for creative work that will support ever-evolving technological, economic and social environments.

We already know workers no longer have the reasonable expectation of spending their adult career in one job. The work environment that will sustain our economic and social environments in the future will be more fluid. Not only will work demands require continuous learning and creativity, but work, itself, will not be the only or maybe even the **primary way citizens contribute to society**. The idea that the transactional world of work where we work our 40 hours and receive pay for our work will be replaced by a **more transformational approach to work** that is more inclusive of ways we contribute to the social good. Especially because computers, artificial intelligence, and new social engagement patterns will replace many workers and work environments, the work-place ecosystem will be supplanted by an **ecosystem of social engagement and contribution**.

Social entrepreneurs are already seen as disruptors to traditional work environments as are gig workers, trend setters, gamers, and internet influencers. Ecosystem engagements supported through and developed by the futures learning ecosystem will be valued and supported for the **social good** they bring. The idea that you could be paid for your artistic contributions, service commitments, or social passions is foreign to an economy that is supported by competition and sustained by hierarchies of wealth that create haves and have-nots. But in the transformational society of the near future, new economies will emerge that value and support these more intangible and less transactional contributions to society.

As the transformational future emerges, we are confronted with redefining and re-visioning what it means to be human and a valuable participant in a civilized society. The learning needs of the future will re-define our identity as societal goals shift from the virtue of selfishness and accumulation of wealth to the celebration of the whole. **Those with a lot of money will no longer be valued more because of their wealth but will be judged by their contributions to our interconnected society.** Just as New Zealand redefined their metrics of social success from GDP to happiness, a futures learning ecosystem will facilitate our social transformation to the next epoch of human existence on earth.

Our goals and passions should not be focused on questions of how do we ensure the piece of pie we get is the biggest, but how do we support the kind of future in which we want to live? Our educative goals, as they were in the modern era, are to support the societal vision of the future—**this future of transformation and connectedness that overcomes the biases and harms we have committed in the name of progress and celebrates our place on this planet as stewards of life.**

Our future continues to unfold, and we believe that it is our time to bring new ways of thinking and innovative tools of leadership to the forefront. As presented in the remaining chapters, there is an emerging leadership style that we have titled Master Capacity Builder for transformational leadership that can be learned and fostered to bring to fruition the kind of world we have so far envisioned.

Chapter 6

Framework For Transformational Leadership

The principles of transformational learning and Master Capacity Builder transformational leadership resonate with us intuitively. The concepts of connecting totally disparate ideas, collaborating with a diversity of people who bring different talents and diverse perspectives, and using new processes to co-create transformational thinking are within our grasp. The challenge is in our ability as transformational leaders to organize, coach, and help ourselves and others build capacities to develop "self-organizing transformative ecosystems" that can adapt quickly to changing conditions and situations. The goal of this chapter is to provide guidance for leaders as they provide the kinds of creative learning ecosystems that allow individuals and organizations to flourish.

The Master Capacity Builder Curriculum project serves as an example of how leaders can support learning ecosystems. Our purpose is to make more accessible the building blocks for a better understanding of these concepts. We want to help leaders gain these skills, put them in practice, and foster the emergence of new ways of seeing and doing in a world of uncertainty, chaos, and complexity in a futures context.

We are bringing together many of the Master Capacity Builder (MCB) documents generated by Rick Smyre, CEO of

Communities of the Future (COTF), and our colleagues over the last couple of decades about transformational learning and leadership. They will be made available by posting them on a sustainable website that will be maintained over time and serve as a companion to this book. An important part of this chapter is to define our terms.

Foundations for Master Capacity Building

Transformational Leadership Development

Most of us are familiar with the term "transformational leadership," and have varying ideas of what it means. For a brief explanation of this leadership style and its origins, you may review Transformational Leadership in the Enterprise – BMC Blogs (Hornay, 2020). For our purposes, we want you to also consider how to develop skills as a Master Capacity Builder transformational leader as described by Smyre and Richardson (2016) in *Preparing for a World That Doesn't Exist – Yet*:

> A Master Capacity Builder is an individual who understands the precepts in this book and uses the ideas and methods to design and facilitate effective transformational processes at the community and organizational levels. An effective Master Capacity Builder must be able to process a wide variety of information and see how things connect while also being open to spontaneous new possibilities as they emerge.
>
> Many traditional planning processes are based on an extension of past best practices borrowed from other organizations and communities. Too often we try to 'fix' existing problems with existing and limited resources without concern for how the society and economy are transforming. As a result, there is an increased level of frustration as we try to make increasingly

obsolete ideas and methods more efficient. Traditional strategic planning processes rarely work in a time of constant change and are a big reason why long-lasting and effective changes rarely happen. If we are to create a truly sustainable civilization as a result of transforming institutions and cities, we must see connections and tackle challenges with fresh ideas and an open and visionary mind; otherwise, we will be doing little more than rearranging deck chairs on a sinking Titanic. (pp. 8-9)

Master Capacity Building for Transformational Ecosystems

The purpose of this and the next chapter is to share resources that we have designed over the years to help leaders learn to develop into Master Capacity Builder transformational leaders able to think and operate in a futures context. These chapters and the Smyre and Richardson (2016) publication contain information as well as provide additional resources that will help you with this endeavor.

Our motivation as leaders in sharing these principles is that we recognize the disruption in our communities and the need we all have to connect with other leaders to tackle new challenges in all arenas including education, workforce, government, business, and so on. Maintaining a climate of creativity and a culture of transformation are essential to the work; yet traditional workplace climates and cultures do not welcome transformative change. Therefore, the work of a Master Capacity builder is holistic as well as individual. It is only in collaboration with others that MCB leadership techniques may be adopted and adapted, resulting in community transformation.

Within these next three chapters, each of 12 related leadership principles is explained and examples are provided to better illustrate the principle and exemplify access points to engage others in your community as you confront a need to make changes or have a desire to improve the status quo. Samples of our developing curriculum workbook/guidebook are introduced and will include the essential terms and concepts (building blocks) that support transformational learning and leadership, along with practical examples, worksheets, and adaptable materials. This workbook could be used, for example, by college faculty who wish to encourage MCB skills-building in students or by business leaders who want to help managers and workers build their skills of the future. The rapidly changing nature of the future of work will demand adaptable workers whose skills have been developed through this Master Capacity Builder curriculum.

The **MCB Transformational Leadership Curriculum** provides a tangible guide for orchestrating and enacting transformational learning ecosystems and understanding the role of the leader in developing and supporting these environments. Although we use the word "curriculum" as a way to provide guidance, we also recognize, as did Bill Pinar (1975) in his classic critique of the curriculum, that the "curricular race-track" we are describing is not static but is designed with flexibility so it can be used by a teacher, by a professional development facilitator in a workplace, or by others interested in facilitating principles of transformative capacity building in multiple community settings (e.g., business, health, transportation, environmental, justice system, etc.). Transformational collaboration is a keystone of Master Capacity Building skills. Examples and activities will be provided to support readers' learning engagements and evolving understandings of futures learning ecosystems.

Ultimately, we want to provide the tools to help leaders guide others to envision an emerging future that is sustainable, collaborative, adaptive, inclusive and filled with diverse, agile, curious, lifelong learners who are the community transformational co-creators. It is within us to collaborate to build a future that we want to see for ourselves and future generations.

And it will necessitate having transformational leaders who can be "and/both" disruptors/healers and help others develop long-term capacities for individual transformation leading to "self-organizing transformative ecosystems" that are resilient in changing conditions and situations.

To help leaders more easily learn these concepts and leadership skills, we also plan to develop brief videos (10 minutes or less) explaining each of the concepts and providing examples. Since podcasts are popular with millennial and digital learners, we are encouraging longer interviews with international futurist Rick Smyre and others who have been the original leaders and thinkers of these Master Capacity Builder concepts through their work with Communities of the Future (COTF). Visit the Communities of the Future Website at https://communitiesofthefuture.org (COTF, nd). The Future Forward College section of the Wake Tech website (https://www.waketech.edu/about-wake-tech/administrative-offices/effectiveness-and-innovation/future-forward) (Wake Tech, nd) chronicles the introduction, development, and impact of Master Capacity Builder skills, as well as other COTF techniques, on college teaching and learning. Some related interviews have been done by Bill Miller with Global Connections Television and can be found at Video Gallery — Global Connections Television (Miller, nd).

All of these resources are being developed with the idea that a facilitator who has learned these MCB principles will be able to encourage collaboration with students/learners and other leaders to be transformational in their thinking and leadership. The key is to help make these principles more accessible to anyone who wants to change the way they work with others in their communities to manage issues (e.g., environmental, homelessness, poverty, health, financial, systemic racism, etc.) more successfully in a rapidly evolving and changing futures context. How can we help leaders tap into and enhance people's receptivity for new ideas, creativity, curiosity, resilience, agility, cross-cultural connections, critical thinking, entrepreneurial, and digital literacy skills? This is the purpose of these chapters.

Related Theories And Writings

Our approach to Master Capacity Building Leadership is relevant for classrooms and boardrooms. While it builds on many of the futures learning foundations already discussed, Master Capacity Building Leadership is especially connected to the learning theory of Connectivism, approaches to group leadership such as Theory U, and assumptions about important futures learning capacities that build on ideas of a growth or continuous learning mindset.

Connectivism

Our work has involved making connections with other related theories such as George Siemens' **connectivism theory**[1] (Siemens, nd). In 2004, Siemens, a pioneer in the development of Massive Open Online Courses (MOOCs), introduced what has been described as "a new theory of learning for the digital age": connectivism (Siemens, 2005). Siemens argued that learning in the digital age is fundamentally different than learning of the past. He proposed that *learning no longer resides within the individual but is hosted by the collective.* Siemens noted as a key tenet of connectivism that *knowing is not as important as the capacity to know.* An emphasis on connections among individuals and information sources and on shared and ever-changing understandings remains an important element of his ongoing work. Implications of connectivism theory include not only transformation in learning environments, but also a transfor-

---

1   (see: https://lidtfoundations.pressbooks.com/chapter/connectivism-a-learning-theo-ry-for-the-digital-age/)

mation in work environments, media, personal knowledge, and instructional design. Connectivism is an especially valuable theory for redefining leadership roles and responsibilities. It emphasizes the importance for leaders and learners to make connections and seek relational understandings as new meanings are explored.

Theory U

Theory U is an approach to leadership strategies for engaging groups of people to challenge their thinking and the status quo. Otto Scharmer's **Theory U** (2009)[2] identifies key principles underlying the dynamics of expanding individual and organizational capacities for change. These strategies can be used to address routine change but are especially valuable for leaders to facilitate navigation through disruptive change requiring transformational approaches. Usually change is planned ("strategic plans for success") or a reaction to a crisis ("fighting fires") from within an established personal or organizational structure (paradigm). Maintaining the integrity of the structure becomes the paramount goal, resulting in a mindset or organizational vision that limits possibilities and solutions to what is "doable"—i.e., what will not overtly disrupt the system. Yet in a time of rapid and unexpected change, such philosophies and practices might be "rearranging the deck chairs" when redirecting the entire ship is the only action that will ensure survival and success.

Theory U identifies the movements required to expand the capacities to understand and respond to the underlying and more pervasive challenges in unfamiliar (and often uncomfortable) collaborations and partnerships. In the video with Otto Scharmer (2018) about his book, *The Essentials of Theory U*[3], he

---

2   See *What is Theory U?* at https://www.toolshero.com/leadership/theory-u-scharmer/
3   See *Essentials of Theory U with Otto Scharmer – Bing Video*, https://www.bing.com/videos/search?q
     =scharmer+video+about+his+book+on+Theory+U&docid=608020193696550489&mid=346861A
     2CF848DCA6672346861A2CF848DCA6672&view=detail&FORM=VIRE

elegantly describes how a group collaborating with each other gets to the point of readiness for transformational thinking.

Cowart's (2020) recent publication on Theory U about presencing and connected listening identifies essential behaviors implicit in Master Capacity Building skills. These skills require willingness to change patterns of behavior in individual, group, and institutional dynamics; and they require a willingness to risk, fail, and continue practicing these transformative relationship skills, among others.

Theory U also has been connected to futures strategies for developing futures literacy (Fleener, 2020). The seven moments of the Theory U approach can be merged with the Expanded Futures Cone to provide a pathway to explore letting go and seeing-as differently along with creating, letting come and presencing. See Figure 6.1 below adapted from Cowart (2020).

Figure 6.1 Seven Moments of Theory U and the Expanded Now

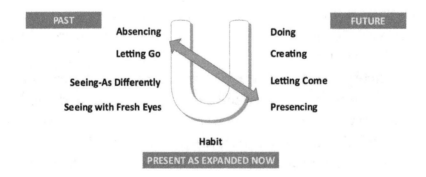

Growth Mindset Nurturing Mindflex

Also, underlying our approach is a connection to Carol Dweck's (2008) **growth mindset** in understanding that humans have a vast capacity for learning and growing. We believe humans have the capacity to learn, unlearn, and uplearn with the appropriate guidance from MCB transformational leaders.

Grant (2021) in *Think Again* writes about the individual work that must be done to allow for exploring our underlying assumptions, unlearning, uplearning (the ability to think and operate at a greater level of complexity) and becoming agile in embracing new perspectives.

Jayne Fleener and Susan Barcinas (2020, p. 633) in "Futurists' relationships with the future: a study of anticipatory meaning-making of ecosystem builders" describe the work of Master Capacity Builders as futurists working to transform social organizations who are "...focused on capacity building, disruption and community for evolving systems revealing an emergentist orientation to the future."

As described in Chapter 1, a growth mindset and mindflex are important skills for transformational learners. Meaningful relationships and supportive environments connect learners and understandings and support emergence of new ideas. Mindflex works together with a growth mindset to enhance capacities to adapt and transform.

Transformational Leadership Principles

The following 12 principles are based on the work of CEO Rick Smyre, Communities of the Future, and as described in the book (2016) co-authored with Neil Richardson, *Preparing for a World That Doesn't Exist—Yet*. These principles underpin a framework of transformational actions and capacity-expanding activities for leaders. Understanding these principles as different from our conventional concepts of leadership is the first step in expanding our own capacities for skillful application of these techniques. As we expand our capacities for understanding and adapting to rapid change, we strengthen our abilities to adapt and thrive in any situation, as well as to help others develop their own skills (personal or professional) for transformation.

Transformational Leadership requires individuals to develop skills beyond those expected from traditional leaders. A Master Capacity builder supports and expands capacities for transformation in the individual and through group dynamics. The skills require thinking in imaginative and innovative ways, abilities to connect totally disparate ideas, people, and processes to co-create transformational thinking, and skill in organizing and building capacities among collaborators for "self-organizing transformative ecosystems" that can adapt quickly to changing conditions and situations.

A Master Capacity Builder is a transformational leader who is focused on creating an innovative culture that encourages participants to expand their capacities for transformational thinking and action. Such an environment enhances participants' abilities to shift their understanding and response to emerging issues, never before experienced, within the context of a new paradigm of a "futures context." A goal of MCB Transformational Leadership is for all participants to become Master Capacity Builders and for leaders to serve as coaches rather than administrators or "leaders" in a hierarchical sense.

Transformative change challenges the underlying assumption of the idea or belief, for example, the ideal of the role of a "leader." Smyre and Richardson (2017, p 61) set out in a chart the principles of a Master Capacity Builder in comparison to a Traditional Builder. Chapter 2 of that book provides more details about Master Capacity Builders for Community Transformation.

The following chart compares attributes of traditional leadership and transformational leadership processes. Each person and group will need to develop the judgment to choose which needs to be emphasized based on each situation and the overall long-term goal of the organization and community.

Table 6.1 Traditional Versus Transformational Leadership

	Traditional Leadership	Transformational Leadership
Short-Term Situation	Takes action	Considers the long-term effects
Long-Term Situation	Predicts a specific outcome	Creates emergent processes
Planning	Strategic planning and linear organization	Adaptive, self-organization and non-linear approaches
Structure	Focuses on standards, rules and hierarchies	Adaptive, self-organization and non-linear approaches
Thinking	Focuses on absolute answers and singular truths	Emphasizes being open to new ideas and choices
Focus	Concerned for how action impacts the leader	Concern for how action impacts the situation and others
Use of the Brain	Emphasizes left brain	Emphasizes integration of right and left brain
Emotional attributes	Emphasizes action, being right, strong opinions	Emphasizes patience, openness to new ideas
Ethics	Concern for "the" truth	Concern for "truths"
Concept of the Individual	Independent and self-sufficient	Interdependent and "connected individuality"
Concept of others	Compares to one's existing beliefs	Embraces diversity and openness of thinking

A **Transformational Leader** may build a small ecosystem of creative participants that interacts with other, similar groups in ever changing and adapting relationships that support the transformation of larger, more complex ecosystems, much as specialized cells in an organism interrelate and interact to support the larger ecosystem of the organism. For example, Fleener and Barcinas (2020, p. 636, 637) describe the work of futurists who are ecosystem builders as emphasizing capacity building and having "...a desire to create new futures and new ideas that expanded the capacity of communities to anticipate and respond to change."

Transformational Leadership is attained through rigorous practice and deep understanding of Master Capacity Building principles. The 12 Key Principles of Transformational Leaders are described below and comprise the fundamental building blocks of the practice.

Employing Adaptive Planning for Complex Adaptive Systems

The principles of complexity and chaos theory are very important for the Master Capacity Builder transformational leader. The capacity for adaptation to radical change is fundamental to the transformational mindset. As a dynamic organization or learning community transforms, it will often do so as a result of unpredictable forces. Strogatz (2020) describes the unpredictability of complex, chaotic systems, especially those that are non-linear, this way: "Chaotic systems are finicky. A little change in how they're started can make a big difference in how they end up. That's because small changes in their initial conditions get magnified exponentially fast" (p. 281). Stirling (2014) explains complex adaptive systems as follows:

*A complex adaptive system is a system which **persists** in spite of changes in the diverse individual components of which it is comprised, in which the interactions between those components are responsible for the persistence of the system, and in which the system itself engages in adaptation or learning. To say that a system is complex is to say that it vacillates between states of order and disorder, without succumbing to either state. To say that such a system adapts* *is to say that it responds to information by changing. Such systems abound. Not only the ant colony and the human body as a whole, but various systems within the body such as the central nervous system and the immune system fall into this category. These are systems that persist in spite of the continual changes of individual components, maintaining coherence and adapting in response to a phenomenal amount of information throughout the lifetime of the organism in which they function.* (p. 5)

Highly isomorphic educational institutions find themselves challenged to respond and adapt as a result of sector constraints and oversight (DiMaggio & Powell, 1983). There are five principles of complexity theory especially relevant to higher education and other highly constrained organizations where adaptive change is difficult. Especially important in these kinds of environments is the ability to connect emerging knowledge with weak signals for adaptive responses through futures generative dialogue (described below) to support complexity and adaptive/emergent action.

- Establishing and creating initial conditions
- Self-organizing
- Emergence
- Constant feedback
- System of interlocking networks

Collaboration Station Example of Futures Generative Dialogue

As an example of adaptive planning, the creation of a free-wheeling "Collaboration Station" during a two-day conference of structured workshops encouraged participants to join into group discussions during any free time they had during the day. Facilitators created the initial conditions of "the no-rules rules", posted lists of topics/concerns generated by the group, encouraged individuals to self-organize outside their accustomed groups, and took notes of ideas/solutions that emerged, provided coaching and constant feedback to strengthen the emerging interlocking networks of participants that bridged disciplines and departments.

The complexity mantra *Think Globally, Act Locally* has provided guidance for how change in even the most constrained sectors of organizations can occur through local efforts to build capacity through the adaptive planning process that supports futures generative dialogue. Through this process, the importance and value of interconnectedness and relationship is honored.

Asking Appropriate Questions

Questions, effectively asked, connect people and ideas in a process of co-creation of a new concept or approach. Leading questions avoid debate and encourage interpretation and insights, while declarative statements often derail discussion and create division among groups. A skilled MCB's questions open the dialogue/creative process to support whatever emerges from a free-flowing discussion. A skilled MCB must be aware of situations and individuals, adaptable to immediate needs of a group, and aware of nuances in the conversation to ask questions that are appropriate to the moment.

Engaging Connective Listening

One's listening habits can reveal whether one is listening to convince or listening to build capacities for exploration. When one listens to compare what is said against what one already believes, what follows may be argument or debate, with participants trying to convince each other that they are right. A Master Capacity Builder always looks to connect new ideas in order to provide a basis for transformational thinking and action. The old methods of debate or discussion are replaced by the principles of "connectivism" in which new ideas and transformational approaches are always evolving.

Connective Listening skills combine with Asking Appropriate Questions with a purpose of connecting disparate ideas within a "futures context" and recognizing emerging connections or patterns. These skills require a shift from requiring singular, standard answers to entertaining emerging connections as the norm, as well as a shift from knowledge-based or traditional truths to emerging knowledge that connects disparate "idea spaces" in continuous learning innovation. Rote learning or planning is replaced with connecting disparate ideas, dynamic critical thinking, and complex reasoning. **Thinking holistically and seeing connections is a major 21st-century skill. The very nature of seeing new connections is the basis for continuous innovation and transformation.**

Other "connectivity points" include connective thinking, which is the ability to make connections among disparate ideas, discoveries, processes, and people. Connective individuality has emerged as a concept important for a society and economy in constant change, since no one individual will have enough knowledge, experience, or time to anticipate the many "connections" that will emerge to propel our society and world into constant transformation. We will need individual connectors to link new and innovative ideas, people, and processes to co-create with others in unpredictable new ways. This relates to the additional skill of Identifying Access Points...finding a point of entry into an emerging system of ideas, people and processes that lead to Interdependence.

Designing and Using Ecosystems

In the past, hierarchies were important to provide a framework within which leaders could make decisions and make choices that would become the standards for all future decisions and choices with the assumption that they would stand the "test of time." However, our era of rampant transformational change requires a different approach, and yesterday's choices will not solve today's problems. MCBs will need to help others expand their capacities to adapt quickly to constant change. To do this, a MCB will need to learn how to 1) Develop networks of different sizes and functional needs; 2) Create interlocking networks that provide the opportunity for participants to deal with complexity; and 3) Design, seed, and facilitate networks and nodes to ensure that any ecosystem that emerges has the capability of providing a "futures context" of some new idea, as well as self-organizing capabilities; these qualities will ensure that those involved with the ecosystem have an expanded capacity for adaptation at any level.

Designing & Utilizing Parallel Processes

The current exponential change, connectedness, and complexity of our societies and economies require transformational leaders to build capacities for transformation through the collaborative development of parallel processes. A community culture that is increasingly open to transformational thinking and action will survive and thrive, especially when parallel processes can be used when traditional systems fail.

MCBs need to develop their own capacities to determine the kinds of networks that are needed, who should be involved (if an open invitation is not feasible), and how to design any network to be self-organizing or spun-off as a project or subsystem when appropriate. Some groups require diversity of experiences and backgrounds, while others may require participants with similar backgrounds and skills. **Comprehensive community transformation requires multiple parallel processes designed to 1) involve interested people in small research and development projects, and 2) have interlocking networks of people to be introduced to emerging trends and "weak sig-**

nals" so that the overall citizenry can expand its ability to have foresight about the future, an important characteristic when exploring emerging issues within a futures context.

Making Spaces for Futures Generative Dialogue and Development

Without the capacity for diverse people to respond without rigid rules and regulations, no organization or community will be able to anticipate change and adapt itself to emerging transformation. **In a transformative ecosystem**, ideas, strategies, and actions will emerge as a result of **"futures generative dialogue."** Quickly connecting and applying disparate ideas, strategies, and actions, and feeding back the results will allow any person, organization, or community to change directions and adapt to a constantly changing context.

Futures generative dialogue is initiated and supported through introducing weak signals and trends into any dialogue so that new ideas and innovations can emerge. Futures Generative Dialogue can be defined as the process of interaction, based on "connective listening" which helps to create new ideas, concepts and methods within a constantly changing "futures context." It replaces the idea of debate, discussion and even traditional dialogue, and builds on new connections that can be developed when new trends, weak signals, and transformational ideas about the future are integrated into the dialogue. By definition, this type of dialogue opens up new thinking. Often, the most important outcomes of Futures Generative Dialogue are those things that could not have been anticipated when entering the dialogue. Smyre and Richardson (2016) indicate:

> The goal of any process of generative development is to establish creative solutions to shorter- and longer-term needs in parallel…while thinking of how ideas and actions will be impacted by future trends. Without thinking in an immediate and futures context at the same time, there can be no generative develop-

ment. Without the ability to listen and see some value in what others are saying, there can be no connections to generate new ideas.... Instead of winning at all costs, the focus of generative development is to find new ways to balance the needs of competing sectors of society, and, in so doing, create purpose for individuals and groups in mutual acts of creation. (p. 43)

Identifying Access Points and Interdependence

Identifying access points and interdependencies is the ability to shift from the core idea of "independence" that emphasizes the unconscious ego needs to be self-sufficient to one of connecting with others or "interdependence." In non-linear, systemic thinking there is a need to identify how multiple factors interconnect. It is important to understand context and how to be interdependent and look for connections in knowledge and ideas that are just emerging. In a futures context, we will no longer be either independent/self-reliant or interdependent, but rather we will operate in and/both.

Supporting Self-Organizing Groups and Deep Collaboration

Deep collaboration uses self-organizing interlocking networks. A shift from organization by hierarchies and command and control to organization by interlocking networks and self-organizing connections as the norm, breaks down silos and operational overlaps within an organization. Smyre and Richardson (2017) state:

> In the future, true collaboration will only occur when those involved sit and dialogue in ways that put themselves in the other person's place and, together, all involved help each other think through the issues of how to develop a set of mutual values, concepts, strategies and actions that are appropriate to the needs [of both] short- or long-term [challenges]. (p. 42–43)

An example of deep collaboration is CNN's description of the process by which two pharmaceutical giants, usually in competition with each other, in 2021 met and brought a partnership to fruition to increase capacity for the Johnson & Johnson COVID-19 vaccine[4].

Example – Self-Organization and PAUSE

An example at Wake Technical Community College (Raleigh, NC) of both the self-organizing principle and the student-led learning principle emerged from the work of a student who identified a problem at the college (students facing poverty, mental health, and substance abuse issues), then reached out to her network of instructors, advisors, friends, and fellow students to help develop solutions. These individuals then reached out to their networks, and so on, until eventually a group of individuals from all levels of the college, including staff, students, faculty, and executive leaders, as well as community advocates, began to implement solutions. The resulting P.A.U.S.E. (Purposeful Acknowledgement, Understanding, and Support for Everyone) project was the result. Recent project efforts have included bringing awareness of food and housing insecurity to campus through a poverty simulation, art exhibit, and documentary and training of more than 50 faculty, staff, and students as mental health first aid responders. This example of a self-organizing deep collaboration resulted in part because of the Master Capacity Building skills the student developed through her participation in the Student Applied Benchmarking program. This program was developed by a group of faculty and students at Wake Technical Community College as an extension of the award-winning Applied Benchmarking pro-

---

4   See ("Merck and Johnson & Johnson vaccine: How the White House convinced two pharmaceutical giants to collaborate" - CNNPolitics) . https://www.cnn.com/2021/03/03/politics/biden-merck-johnson--johnson-dpa/index.html

gram created by Wake Tech President Emeritus Dr. Stephen Scott for college employees (Barton & Moore, 2019). In both the student and employee versions, participants are encouraged to find a way to improve the college by identifying a need, benchmarking an expert in the field, and creating a proposal for funding. Appendix F is an example of how this process can be integrated into any classroom setting.

Sustaining Self-Organizing Transformative Ecosystems and Cells

Smyre and Richardson (2017) describe how to help groups self-organize into transformative ecosystems (cells and nodes) and describe the building of a "pH Ecosystem" in healthcare as an example. The MCB leader who has established self-organizing groups and supported deep collaboration needs to sustain support throughout transformative processes both internally at individual and organizational levels, and externally as environmental conditions continue to change. Ecosystem builder projects such as those sponsored by the Kauffmann Foundation emphasize the importance of continued support for innovation and emergence to avoid extinguishing creativity and returning to status quo.

Creating Transformative Cells

One of the challenges of organizational or systems change is where to begin. One of the skills a MCB needs to develop is how to create cells of innovation within existing structures. Transformative cells are the building blocks of Transformative Ecosystems. They are self-organizing units focused on a new transformational idea such as Transformational Learning.

Composed of individual "nodes" (individual small units who develop different transformative ideas), interact and connect with aligned nodes over core cell concepts, building capacities for each idea. As the ideas evolve, persons involved look for connections among those ideas to help foster and co-create different "self-organizing transformative ecosystems." It is through the creation of this new collaborative mechanism that "capacities for transformation" will evolve quickly and ensure that people, ideas, and processes adapt as conditions and concepts are transformed.

Gamestop Example of Transformative & Interactive Cells

In the investing world, an example of this principle occurred in January 2021, when the traditional short selling of stocks in a company perceived to be failing (Gamestop) had drastically different results than intended by the short sellers. News about the company, a favorite with video gamers, was mentioned on the Reddit Forum/Wall Street Bets, and Reddit followers used Robinhood, a free trading pioneer app, to explode the company's stock to a 400% gain in one week, closing out the month with a total gain of 1625%. The self-organizing Reddit group (transformative cell) caused major losses for the short sellers betting against it, as well as for Robinhood, as it had to back the stock. This unprecedented action sent ripples across all markets and their regulators—i.e., the stock market ecosystem. Unpredictable, unplanned—the group self-organized, focused, and acted to disrupt the status quo of short-sell practices.

Higher Education Example of Transformative Cells

Small groups of colleagues across two different IHEs in Texas and North Carolina were identified and supported by their college presidents as transformative cells for change. The two presidents recognized the power of these small cells of innovation and decided to create spaces and opportunities for the two groups to meet regularly to discuss Future Forward topics, connecting via video conferencing tools to exchange ideas.

Supporting Transdisciplinary Thinking and Interaction

Connecting totally disparate ideas and areas within a futures context is part of supporting transdisciplinary thinking and interaction. Business, learning, and societal structures are strongly organized in groups of similar qualities and objectives. While efficient, such systems also create a "silo" effect, where diversity of thought or experience is discouraged and interactions with "others" is deemed irrelevant. Transdisciplinary interactions expand essential connections and capacities for other essential MCB skills.

Example of Adaptive Planning to Support Transdisciplinary Thinking

Focus groups for strategic/adaptive planning or course design at a college include all stakeholders, including students, faculty, staff, administrators, and trustees. The diverse points of view will provide more data as well as more creative ideas to transform the learning experience.

Supporting Transformational Learning

Smyre and Richardson (2016) describe transformational learning as: "the concept of learning that integrates the need to expand knowledge (to include trends and weak signals), ask appropriate questions within a futures context, and connect diverse and disparate ideas for the purpose of continuous innovation" (p. 215). We have described elsewhere in this book how transformative learning is vital to addressing the challenges of a society in transition. There are particularly useful knowledge, skills, aptitudes and values of futures thinking that can be applied as our society faces this fundamental shift.

Master Capacity Builders engage others with a variety of skills that connect concepts and activities that engender transformational learning. Several examples of this will be explored in chapter 7.

Identifying Weak Signals and Emerging Trends

The ability to identify weak signals and emerging trends and be able to understand their potential impact are important skills for a MCB in creating a futures context. Weak signals are like the faint signals on radar that become stronger as they get closer. They are emerging ideas, inventions, discoveries and innovations that are not yet trends but have the potential to impact local areas within 3–5 years. A recognition of weak signals can inform any process through which learning geared at coping with or creating the future is taking place.

Weak Signals and the Coronavirus

The coronavirus pandemic provided us with many examples of weak signals and emerging trends that directly affected our lives. The idea that we could rapidly develop a vaccine for the coronavirus (weak signal although one heard round the world) was reported in March/April 2020 at the beginning of the pandemic. Most people did not believe (and some still don't) that effective vaccines could be developed within 2020, since standard procedures require five years or more for vaccine development and testing. Nonetheless, the production, emergency authorization, and deployment of effective coronavirus vaccines is a reality in 2020-21, although many challenges have occurred and continue to emerge. Today we understand that the development of the vaccines in a shorter period occurred because of the deep collaboration of varying scientists across the world and the connections of disparate ideas and recognition of weak signals made by them.

Schools, colleges and universities, as well as retail services and medical communities, recognized early into the pandemic the need to go either fully remote or hybrid, which is an emerging trend for the future post-pandemic way of life. Businesses responded to the weak signal that became an emerging trend by offering customers safe, remote, in-home, and outdoor experiences and selling products/services that related to those opportunities necessitated by the pandemic. Healthcare recognized the emerging trend of telemedicine that will likely be more accepted (by patients and insurers) in the future.

Summary

The MCB Leadership principles are represented below. Rather than listed in a linear way, the skills and dispositions of MCB leaders are embedded within a complex plane that combines actions, skills, and orientations to the future. Supporting transdisciplinary thinking includes and embeds challenges of supporting transformational learning, exploration of and skills for identifying weak signals, and development of futures literacy capacities of workers, as discussed in chapter 5. Supporting and sustaining self-organization and continuous change through transformation, MCB skills include asking the right questions, connective listening and supporting futures generative dialogue. And at an organizational perspective, MCB strategies include adaptive planning, designing ecosystems and supporting cells of transformation, and creating parallel processes.

Figure 6.2 Master Capacity Builder's Toolkit

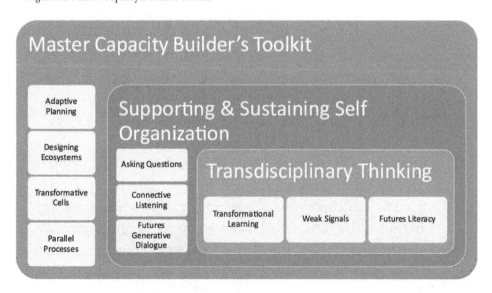

These skills provide guidance for the MCB to establish and create the initial conditions for change and unleash the potential for emergence and self-organization. Constant feedback and connections both within the organization and with others is important to develop the capacities of the organization to continually be renewed, creative, and adaptive.

The next chapter will explore some specific examples of how these principles have been used. It will serve as a guidepost for those who see the need for transformational futures within their organizations and lives.

Chapter 7

Framework For Transformational Leadership

While many of the examples herein are designed to support the work of leaders, they can also be applied to classrooms and those whose leadership realm is in support of futures learning. Educators, futurists, community leaders, business leaders and policymakers will benefit from these examples which extend the conversations from the previous chapter. Through these activities, transformational leadership and learning converge to develop a perspective or social fabric for an emerging world of transformation where existing values and ways of doing things are challenged and replaced and leadership skills are enhanced to support transformational learning, including creativity and futures thinking, within their organization.

The Master Capacity Builder strategies work together with the MCB Toolkit as action-oriented approaches to supporting futures learning and within and for organizations and the people who comprise them. While there is overlap with the toolkit of MCB understandings, these strategies provide important and useful actionable ways to support innovation, creativity and sustained change for a transformational world.

MCB Strategies To Leading Transformation

Adaptive Planning for Complex Adaptive Systems

The emergence of insight, intuition, imagination and innovation are the basis for adaptive planning. No longer either/or—we need a different worldview based on interlocking networks and systems, connections, parallel processes and multiple answers—a world of and/both. Adaptive planning assumes that one cannot predict what is emerging and that what needs to be done is to develop processes and interlocking networks to build "capacities for transformation" that provide the ability to "adapt" quickly so that any interested individual, group, network or community can pivot and respond in real time to whatever happens on the horizon.

As the pace of change accelerates, networks and ecosystems of people, business and other organizations and communities need to be designed for rapid, speedy adaptability. Adaptive planning complements strategic planning and is an essential leadership skill that supports the emergence of new concepts and methods that are effective and transformational for the longer run.

Smyre and Richardson (2016) explain,

> [T]he longer the timeframe of planning, the more ambiguity will exist and the more we need new techniques of anticipating uncertainty. If one looks twenty years ahead, one needs to look for weak signals before they become trends and to learn how to frame and seed the creation of new capacities that will help ensure any organization or community will be able to transform itself. Again, we need the key capacity of seeing connections among apparently disparate factors. Instead of trying to identify specific outcomes at the beginning of any process, adaptive

planning emphasizes the creation of small groups of committed people to study various trends and areas of community life and then begin to generate new ideas from the dialogue that ensues. Outcomes emerge from the "futures generative dialogue." (p. 46)

With that in mind, the following short acronym, D.I.C.E., can be used as a framework of thinking for adaptive planning for the future that can be applied in classrooms, learning communities, and interlocking networks (see Workbook, Appendix G, for complete worksheet).

D -- DESIGN
I -- IDENTIFY
C -- CONNECT
E -- EMERGE

The DICE approach has been used with students as well as by leaders to communicate and facilitate the adaptive planning process. Rolling the DICE in this context reinforces that, unlike traditional strategic planning processes that are linear and have clear beginning and ending periods, DICE is a continuous process.

The worksheet in Appendix A is a Progress Chart for Building Capacities for Transformation that helps in assessing growth in these leadership qualities.

Asking Appropriate Questions

Consider the types of questions that can open minds and generate creativity. Depending on the topic and scope of discussion, this skill requires mindfulness, attention, and mental agility.

A MCB might ask questions to:
- determine what is happening.
- connect diverse people and ideas.

- introduce a new concept.
- help create positive tension in a group growth situation.
- build modules of innovations.
- increase the capacity of risk for an individual or group.
- build networks.
- help others see complex issues.
- resolve conflict.
- open doors to new thinking.
- encourage quiet participants to contribute ideas.
- rethink a decision.
- overcome obstacles and objections.
- help people think at a higher level.
- encourage strong-willed people to listen to others.
- shift from reforming change to transforming change.
- build parallel processes of strategic and eco-planning.

A MCB who knows how to ask the right questions, and when to ask the question, encourages thoughtfulness, creativity, community, wonder, and commitment. Sincerely asked, the MCB leader learns more by listening to the answers than telling participants what to think or do. Asking the right questions is not done in the spirit of manipulation, where the leader expects a certain answer, but is done in the spirit of adventure, openness and exploration.

Connective Listening/Creative Connections

A "connective listener" builds a conversation from a point of agreement (whether 1%, 50%, or 100%), and builds an "ecosystem" of dynamic, creative knowledge/understanding by recognizing emerging connections and broadening the areas of agreement. Using the Transformational Leadership techniques of creative connections such as "and/both" and "linear/non-linear thinking," the MCB always seeks areas of agreement (common ground) on which to build new ideas, methods, and parallel processes. By identifying, reinforcing, and connecting common ground, a leader can create a culture of collaboration instead of debate and disagreement.

Being a connective listener is related to being able to ask appropriate questions. As questions are answered, it is imperative that the leader listen with sincere interest and seek the commonalities and connections across ideas. No idea is ever rejected and no matter how seemingly obscure, comments and ideas from participants often have seeds of genius that need to be nurtured through connections and understanding.

Creative Connections: And/Both (vs. Either/Or)

In the emerging interdependent society and economy, many factors will interact. Newly emerging knowledge will need to be connected, and many solutions will be appropriate at any one time, depending on the situation, leading toward a need for the principle of "**and/both.**" And/Both encourages a different self-organizing concept of interlocking networks and systems, connections, parallel processes, and multiple answers, and it requires an openness to unconventional connections.

A too-rigid solution set for any discussion will limit the creativity and adaptability of the responses. For example, in a community development setting, traditional housing designs could be reimagined if planning occurred with a diverse group of participants, including architects, environmentalists, and differently-abled residents. The results might reflect the "and/both" approach as seen in the Universal Design of new buildings. Older buildings often require retrofitting to add ramps to areas of stairs or steps to improve accessibility. A more inclusive solution in this case might be to build sloping walkways instead of steps to provide equal access to everyone, regardless of abilities.

Creative Connections: Linear and Non-Linear Capacity Building

To build toward transformational thinking when constructing a parallel process or problem solving, a MCB will encourage collaborators to participate in an adjustment from linear (either-or) thinking to non-linear thinking (considering multiple answers according to each situation). By shifting between the styles of thinking, participants become more comfortable with ambiguity and uncertainty. Smyre and Richardson (2016) note:

> Once a new idea is developed using connective thinking, new strategies become important to implement the idea. This requires a combination of non-linear, connective thinking to build effective parallel processes, and linear thinking to make sure effective actions are taken with accountable outcomes defined. (p. 28)

For example, as the dean responsible for a tutoring lab you notice from the monthly usage reports that fewer students are using the lab. Do you analyze the data to determine which demographics have decreased their use and ask your team to market the lab to them in the future (linear thinking) or do you bring together a diverse team knowledgeable about the tutoring lab and its users and ask an open-ended question: Why do you think the usage of the tutoring lab has decreased for the past several months (non-linear thinking)? Or do you use both strategies (linear and non-linear thinking)? A MCB learns the skills to do both and understands the benefits of non-linear thinking although it may not be the most time efficient in the short run.

Identifying Access Points and Interdependence

Identifying access points is the ability to recognize a place of connection to begin to talk about transformational thinking and action. Smyre and Richardson (2016) note,

"A key skill for any Master Capacity Builder Transformational Leader is to be able to identify an access point where a new idea, concept or method can be seeded in the thinking and activities of people, processes, organizations, and communities." (p. 94)

In order to facilitate the process of identifying access points, connective listening and appropriate questions are useful. Together, access points, connective listening and asking appropriate questions can help to 1) introduce a weak signal; 2) seed a new idea when identifying an access point; and 3) move to a deeper collaboration. Interdependence is a relationship among ideas and people. It is helpful to discern how a new idea or weak signal can be seeded by asking a question, quoting a thought leader, or recommending an article or podcast.

For example, a conversation took place between an executive team member and a college president who asked for the name of a speaker for a community meeting. The team member recognized an opportunity (access point) to recommend Rick Smyre as a presenter who could talk about transformational thinking and Master Capacity Builder principles. This later resulted in a creative collaboration between the college and community members.

Moving In and Out

The ability to adapt individual work styles and processes to those of other individuals in order to work effectively as a group to accomplish tasks involves building capacities for Moving In and Out. Significant or transformative change is most often the result of collective efforts. Networks whose members are able to establish workflows that maintain momentum while simultaneously collecting input from multiple nodes (individuals or small groups) have the potential to support, trigger, or reinforce transformation. Master Capacity Builders know that in order for complex adaptive systems to flourish, members must be flexible and responsive to the needs of other members. This requires more than just finding a mutually agreeable time for a dialogue. "Moving in and out" involves building a deeper awareness of and appreciation for the needs of others, while also being self-aware and able to assert one's own needs.

Moving in and out is a function of complex adaptive systems that may relate to self-similarity across scales. Looking at the individual level of accomplishment offers a reflection of the collective, and vice versa. Moving in and out also functions on psychological scales where understanding the mental and physical health of an organization is related to the health of individuals. Rather than a top-down perspective of leadership, MCB leaders understand they need to continually shift their focus across organizational and individual levels.

Parallel Processes

To help communities or organizations recognize a need for new ways of doing and acting there is a need for simultaneous efforts that must be developed in parallel. A community/organization will have three types of people: 1) those struggling to keep their heads above water, 2) those who have learned to adapt to changing conditions, and 3) those who are open to new ideas and enjoy being involved at the cutting edge in research and development. Any systemic approach to prepare a community for a different kind of society and economy needs to have parallel processes that will involve similar people in one process (due to differences in educational and experience background) and diverse people in a different process (when a new idea needs the diversity of experiences and backgrounds).

Comprehensive community transformation requires multiple parallel processes that will 1) involve interested people in small research and development projects, and 2) have interlocking networks of people be introduced to emerging trends and "weak signals" so that the overall citizenry can expand its ability to have foresight about the future...a characteristic important to respond to emerging issues within a futures context.

We are in an age of systems that require leaders to design parallel processes to deal with different needs simultaneously, e.g. focusing on short-run interests and longer-run capacities and interests at the same time. For example, a Boomers Collaborative being developed in Austin, Texas[1] is using a deep collaborative parallel process to address the shortage of housing being recognized throughout the United States. This innovative group of leaders is encouraging others to think futuristically and to collaboratively develop with boomers, businesses, artists, entrepreneurs, and urban planners an environmentally sustainable living and working space for boomers, in parallel with traditional housing.

Reflecting and Connecting

Applying Siemen's theory of Connectivism to Transformative Leadership involves examining one's own actions with the goal of continuous learning. Master Capacity Builders spend time reflecting and connecting in order to process new knowledge fully and to gain additional insights. Increasing self-awareness is a goal of reflection that can be supported by reflecting first as an individual and then spending time connecting with others (who share their own individual and often diverse reflections) in order to gain a broader collective understanding of an issue or event.

For example, if a group works together on a task, it will be important for those involved to spend time reflecting on what aspects of their work together were most helpful and what could be changed, improved or transformed. Individuals will ask themselves "What can be learned from this experi-

---

1   See http://www.austintexas.gov/edims/document.cfm?id=249153 and at https://www.boomerscollaborative.org/ .

ence?" with the goal of making changes in the future. Then, as a group, individuals will share their own learnings with each other. Adapting to the style of a "futures generative dialogue," no one's insights are wrong or invalid. Everyone plays a part in bringing a different perspective to the table so that the group as a whole can co-create ideas for moving forward. Each MCB skill development activity could include "community reflections" to allow for co-creating new ideas. A template for supporting this approach can be found in Appendix F.

Seeding New Ideas

It is important to help ourselves and others become more comfortable with listening for weak signals and emerging trends and gain the skill of seeding new ideas. How do we help others and ourselves get out of "comfort zones" that mire us into a stale way of thinking? Our traditional way of thinking focuses us on absolute answers and singular truths. As Master Capacity Builder transformational leaders, we want to seed new ideas by asking appropriate questions such as, how does the issue at hand connect to the article we read earlier today? What idea or new project comes into your mind as a result of these three disparate factors?

As an example, a MCB group leader can ask people to form groups of three and each share an idea related to the issue at hand and seed a new idea resulting from their futures generative dialogue. Those small groups can seed their ideas into those of other groups and generate connected new ideas and so on to co-create more new ideas leading to transformative ecosystems and transformational solutions.

Unlearning and Uplearning

It is clear in the field of education and the workforce that due to the evolving changes in our world, we need to be lifelong learners and to help others unlearn ways of obsolete thinking, leading, and doing that no longer are effective. It's important to understand that there is no one answer or solution to our "big" issues, like climate change, and that no one person can possibly have all the knowledge necessary to tackle such challenges. Once we unlearn these various "truths" or underlying assumptions, we can uplearn, at a higher level of complexity, new ways of thinking, leading and doing.

Technology provides accessible ways of understanding the unlearning and uplearning process. Every new upgrade of technology requires unlearning and uplearning. Moving from a location-specific telephone to a cell phone, is one example. Any computer system—phone or laptop—usually requires unlearning certain actions and learning new ones. To develop the coronavirus vaccines, traditional approaches to vaccine development were unlearned and faster methods of development and distribution were uplearned, and the uplearning continues.

Sometimes unlearning requires more than refining our thinking to adapt to changes but may entail entirely new models that replace the old. New Zealand's shift from Gross National Product (GNP) as a measure of economic success to happiness is an example of unlearning ways of measuring success that rely on production metrics and profits, with an underlying assumption of bigger is better, to a more sustainable and diffuse concept of happiness. The country is now uplearning how to measure happiness in meaningful ways as a metric of societal success.

Conclusions

The MCB strategies are summarized below.

Figure 7.1 Master Capacity Builder Strategies

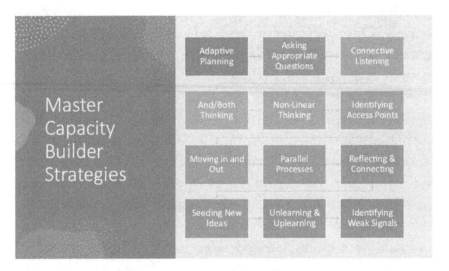

The examples provided offer insights into how the MCB can use these strategies within the MCB Toolkit framework to support transformational learning within organizations and society. The next chapter continues to build on to the leadership strategies for transformational learning at a societal level.

Chapter 8

Engaging Strategies for Transformation

In this chapter we explore various occasions for building social capacities and identifying opportunities for disruption and regeneration through a Master Capacity Builder transformational leadership lens. We are living in a period of major disruption brought on by the global pandemic, racial inequities, demographic changes and declining birth rates, environmental challenges, and new cultural trends, including a desire for "cancel culture." The MCB curriculum provides opportunities for engaging our diverse communities to have courageous dialogue about co-creating a new, more inclusive future using parallel processes with the existing norms.

Examples of emerging disruptive trends can be seen across all sectors of our culture and communities:

- Economic: bitcoin and other forms of digital currency (regulated or unregulated; global economies); recognition of deep interdependencies; antitrust movement; outdated electric grid infrastructure; renewable energy sources; 5G; e-commerce; digital identity/biometric authentication; cybersecurity
- Societal inequities: Black Lives Matter, LGBTQI+, and #MeToo movements; Labor unrest; pandemic deaths greatest among vulnerable populations; inade-

quate health access for vulnerable populations; majority of Latinx and other low-income students attend least well-funded institutions--public community colleges; housing shortages

- Medical: telemedicine; inequities in medical research and services; supply chain vulnerabilities; pandemic surge = inadequate hospital/ ICU beds and equipment; robotics and artificial intelligence; use of quantum computers in healthcare sector
- Transportation: autonomous and electric vehicles/airplanes; electric charging stations; high-speed rails; infrastructure transformation; internet of things (IoT)/ connectivity
- Agriculture/communities/safety: climate change; pollution; digital technologies; meat 2.0 alternatives; drones; market disruptions; protection of critical infrastructure

To address the transformational needs of society, each of these sectors needs to be considered. MCB Leadership is needed to achieve these kinds of comprehensive and simultaneous changes. Below are specific areas where MCB Leadership is especially needed.

Transforming the Teaching/Learning Paradigm

As we have described in the first chapters of this book, we need to rethink what it means to know and do. If we disrupt traditional teaching/learning roles and structures by moving from didactic teaching to collaborative, student-directed learning communities with faculty serving as transformational coaches, we may generate a new teaching dynamic that empowers students to co-create a learning experience that is inclusive of their interests, goals, and academic requirements. While transformative teaching/learning is happening in some locations, entire ecosystems, from pre-K to college, have not transformed.

Students who were involved in one—and only one—style of learning in early grades find obstacles when confronted with additional critical thinking requirements in high school or college, and their capacities for adaptation and independent analysis are woefully deficient. Although the coronavirus pandemic provided an opportunity for transformation when most learning was moved from the face-to-face environment to the online environment, the educational community as a whole has not been prepared to make a radical shift. Faced with the challenge of creating some stability for their students, most educators adapted traditional forms of learning to make them fit, as much as possible, with a new paradigm.

Despite the resistance to adaptation when faced with massive disruption, the educational community as a whole has undergone a process of change that may engender a greater willingness to break with the past and to develop new methods of collaboration with students and each other to determine how to best cultivate Transformational Learning in the future. As alluded by Winston Churchill: Never underestimate the value of a good crisis.

Transforming the Community Development Paradigm

By disrupting hierarchical "community leadership" traditions, communities can build inclusive, diverse action groups that foster collaboration and creative enrichment throughout all levels of community life. Smyre has introduced this transformational model in Georgia and Canada, while Neil Richardson has developed strategic/adaptive planning initiatives for communities as diverse as Washington, D.C. and West Africa that fostered beneficial community diversity and involvement. See the website Emergent Action (https://emergentaction.com/neil-richardson-dc/) for more information.

Transforming the Economic Paradigm

Crises and technology are effectively morphing world and local economies into shapes unrecognizable and unmanageable by past operational strategies. Consider the Robin-Hood/Reddit (nontraditional) to the traditional short selling of Gamestop[1] or the challenges and initiative resulting from the increased use of bitcoins and other cryptocurrencies, and Non-Fungible Tokens (NFTs). These initiatives may feel like freefalls but could be opportunities for agile, adaptable planning, providing a responsive structure that offers some stability and support for the future.

Transforming the Workforce

Factory models throughout communities must be transformed. Past education factories produced specialized workers trained and equipped to function as specialized components in well-developed economic "factories"—white or blue collar—that supported a well-established economic system. The factory pipeline (starting in primary school) was a one-way street. That pipeline is in pieces and that metaphor is obsolete. A new metaphor—a new language building on the reality of a transformed global economy in the midst of endless flux—is being created and put into practice to develop parallel processes as the old industrial model decays. Changes are already happening, but are they enough? Are they transformative? New, adaptable, and transformative connections are established when participants think and plan through transformational collaboration among those with Master Capacity Builder skills.

---

1 See https://www.cnbc.com/2021/01/30/gamestop-reddit-and-robinhood-a-full-recap-of-the-historic-retail-trading-mania-on-wall-street.html; Li, Yun. "Gamestop, Reddit, and Robinhood: a Full Recap of the l Retail Trading Mania on Wall Street." CNBC, 30 Jan. 2021)

Transforming Workforce Development

The Master Capacity Builder transformational leadership principles that we discuss in previous chapters can be used to engage groups interested in workforce development and preparing students and workers for the future world of work. The use of technology, robots, and artificial intelligence in the workplace is transforming how people work and the jobs that are available for them. This rapid deployment of new technologies is disrupting workforce development in communities and how we prepare ourselves for new opportunities. The changing world of work is increasingly requiring partnerships between education, business, philanthropic organizations, governmental and other community entities. Disruptions prior to the coronavirus pandemic included a loss of jobs, increased unemployment, a need for upskilling and retraining, and a mismatch between changing industry job skills needed and the preparedness of people looking for work. The pandemic heightened these challenges because of even greater loss of jobs due to service industry (e.g., restaurants, salons, accounting, teaching, etc.) lockdowns, closures or downsizing affecting primarily low-income wage earners but also disrupting middle-income earners.

Additionally, there have been regional differences in impact on the workforce; while some regions have thrived, others have retrenched or even been decimated. The pandemic has spotlighted these community workforce challenges and exacerbated them with major labor disruptions. On the other hand, other communities have prospered economically and grown, especially those with thriving technology industries. A 2020 comprehensive report by MIT, *The Work of the Future, Building Better Jobs in an Age of Intelligent Machines*, discusses these and many other issues confronting the workforce now and in the future.

Our interest as educators focuses on preparing students for

the future of work and helping them gain the skills necessary to prosper in a rapidly changing landscape. One concept is clear-- all of us will need to be lifelong learners as our changing world will require us to remain nimble as we constantly adapt to a transforming culture and world. We have definitely learned the need to adapt during this unprecedented pandemic and to create new ways of living and collaborating.

A lifelong learner is described as someone who is open to new opportunities, curious, and willing to engage in reskilling for job transitions and conceptual transformations. A January 2021 survey by the Pew Research Center indicates that two-thirds of those unemployed, temporarily laid off, or furloughed stated they have seriously considered changing their occupation or field of work because they are pessimistic about job prospects. One concern is that communities will have to prepare to transition workers into new jobs, especially Blacks, Latinx (Hispanics), women, and low-wage earners, including younger workers, who have been disproportionately affected by the pandemic. Another concern is that those who are unemployed may be reluctant to participate in reskilling and upskilling necessary for job transitions. McKinsey & Company (2021) in "The Future of Work after COVID-19" indicates that up to 25% more workers than previously projected will need to change occupations and will need upskilling for the new jobs that will be available.

Transforming by Reimagining Infrastructure

Master Capacity Builders will most certainly be needed in the near future to practice adaptive planning skills in addressing infrastructure concerns across the United States and other parts of the world. The pandemic of 2020 has brought into clearer focus several critical weaknesses in the system that futurists have been discussing for some time. The urban food distribution system, for example, has been described by researchers as "fragile" (Clark, Conley, & Raja, 2020). Problems with power grids are not limited to Texas, though the February 2021 disaster in that state provided a preview of what can be expected nationwide if substantial change is not made. Toilet paper shortages became a national joke, but shortages in personal protective equipment, ventilators, and other medical supplies turned deadly worldwide. At this point, action is a necessity, not an option. While it may be easiest to try to modify and adapt existing systems to conserve time and money, *transformative change* in our infrastructure is the only way to avoid continuing stopgap measures indefinitely.

Transforming Education (all levels)

The 21st Century leadership skills needed (e.g., capacity-building and effective communication skills, creativity, curiosity, resilience, agility, cross-cultural connections, critical thinking, entrepreneurial, and digital literacy skills, etc.) will increasingly require educational institutions to pivot and partner with government, industry, and other educational entities. The pandemic has revealed how vulnerable our educational institutions are to major setbacks. The focus of educational institutions has been to survive during the pandemic and those that have thrived are the exception. Enrollment in higher education has declined, especially first-time freshmen and community college enrollment, as reported in 2020 by the National Clearinghouse Research Center and in 2021 by the *New York Times* at https://nyti.ms/3mfNqww. And secondary education has struggled to keep students engaged, especially remotely.

However, post pandemic there will be incredible opportunities for reimagining and growth in the higher education sector and for innovation in secondary education. **The higher education sector will need to prepare itself now for the profound**

foundational changes that will be necessary to educate students for the future world of work and to motivate people to stay in school and seek further learning.

An example of the immense--especially in scale and depth--changes required for community colleges is described in the Education Strategy Group (2020) document, "A More Unified Community College." These visionary experts amplify what community colleges will need to do to align academic credit and workforce non-credit programs to break down silos within academics, student services, and administrative/operations to better prepare students for the future world of work. A new framework of alignment and the incremental processes necessary are described and the Education Study Group (2020) authors note:

> Implementing this framework will not be easy. It will require **transformational leadership** at all levels to enact the vision. There will need to be strong coordination and collaboration among stakeholders, particularly faculty and staff, to implement the changes. It will require an understanding of policies and processes, a commitment to outcomes and accountability, and a reprioritization of resources. Cultural norms must be identified and modified. External stakeholders, such as employers and states, will need to support and prioritize the work. (p. 10)

The new framework for alignment recommended in the report is a recognition that the current structure of community colleges with separate academic and non-academic programs is not serving students well for a future that is constantly evolving with new technologies and jobs that will require different skills and preparation. The Education Strategy Group report (2020, p. 26) highlights examples of this transformational work being done at community colleges throughout the country that are consistent with many of the MCB Leader strategies. For example, one of the recommendations is: Be willing to think outside of traditional structures to meet existing and future demand. A few examples of this include the Ascend Institute at Dallas College, which will serve as a one-stop for employers wanting to work with the district; the new Business Solutions venture at PGCC [Prince George Community College], which will take a consultative approach to innovate and quickly respond to industry needs; and the Future of Work Center at Monroe Community College, which will provide flexible space that can be rapidly retooled for new forms of training with industry partners.

These are only a few examples of how Master Capacity Builder principles can be used to facilitate transformation in various sectors and connect to emerging opportunities for capacity building in a world of increasing disruption, complexity and rapid change.

Forward Looking Thoughts (Disruption & Regeneration)

It is hard to imagine the multiplicity of our futures. Our brains are not conditioned to do so. That is one of the challenges for a different kind of future that will require us to think holistically. We say "the Future" as if there were only one, and that provides an illusion of stability, structure, and inevitability that is just that: an illusion. When confronted with the anxiety-producing uncertainties of day-to-day life, managing the small-scale disruptions often blinds us to the larger-scale changes that drive and form one future or another. Until we are comfortable acknowledging and discussing potential outcomes of multiple possible futures (futures-generative conversations), we will struggle to recognize, let alone build, new paradigms for ourselves and our communities. Until then, we are at risk of obsolescence: behind the curve, beneath the wave.

Through study, practice, and collaboration, we can build our capacities for recognizing and analyzing change early (Weak Signals and future forward conversations); effective deep listening and collaboration (moving in and out and reflection); and understanding continuous transformation as something altogether different from continuous improvement (unlearning and uplearning). Since our capacities for growth are limited only by our fear of the unfamiliar and change, Master Capacity Building of oneself or in coaching others is an endless creative effort. Community ecosystems that are transformational and transformative foster small events (self-organizing groups) and transform larger systems (community, economic, educational). Master Capacity Builders mindfully effect the shift of paradigms which are better equipped to survive huge disruptors such as pandemics, climate change, economic disasters, and shifts in the organization of social systems.

Conclusions

We believe that the Master Capacity Builder transformational leadership principles, tools, and strategies discussed herein will embolden leaders to collaborate in developing a culture of experimentation and increasing opportunities for reskilling/upskilling for job transitions. Preparing ourselves to build our capacities to thrive in our new world is one of the reasons we have been so eager to share these Master Capacity Builder principles that we have been learning and putting into practice.

If change is inevitable, why do individuals resist change, even when they do not intend to? Perhaps it is because change requires mental effort. The human brain must form new neural pathways to build frameworks for understanding novel concepts. Effort must be expended to assimilate fresh knowledge with prior understandings. With the many changes the world has experienced since the COVID-19 pandemic, a longing for something that feels safe and familiar is natural. Yet it is clear that a better world, a less flawed one, can only be created if change is embraced, both individually and collectively. Those with the will to undertake this effort must encourage one another to continue learning, collaborating, sharing, and leading. As educators committed to transformational change, we are hopeful that the ideas shared will help to further this worthy cause. For those willing to join us in this work, we offer some final questions for reflection as both a summary and call to action.

Navigating the Ecosystem of Learning for the Second Enlightenment

What can studying historical beginnings and endings teach about current transformations?

What thought changes have played a role in societal transformation so far and how might changes in ideas about economics, politics, technology, and religion increase capacity for transformational change?

What changes in thought would be required to shift from a more competitive society to a more cooperative one? How would this shift impact future possibilities?

How can individuals move from being in isolation to being in community? How would communities be changed as a result?

Why is it important to see differences as opportunities instead of oppositions? How would this change in thinking lead to progress?

How might seeing the role of nature differently lead to new ways of engaging with natural resources?

How would a shift in momentum from moving to a more global economy to moving towards a more local economy impact society and the distribution of wealth?

What does it mean to love life more than money? How can this disposition be developed? What changes would result if society as a whole developed this disposition?

What is the difference between wisdom and information accumulation? How does a traditional view of metaphysics shape underlying assumptions about the way the world works? What role does language play in limiting or influencing thought?

How might the world change if we all could love enemies as well as neighbors?

Ponderings for Learning in an Age of Transformation

How does the current pandemic and the crossroads it represents relate to the pandemic of 13th and 14th century Europe? How can past transformations illuminate present changes? How will ethical questions created by technological developments be answered? What role will teaching and learning play in shaping the answers to these questions? How do current educational systems create or reinforce a "third rail" that is lethal to creative thought?

How does the myth of individual autonomy and accomplishment impede collective efforts? What is lost when education focuses on accumulating knowledge rather than developing ingenuity as a result of the myth of progress? How does the myth of competition reinforce the myth of individual autonomy and accomplishment? How does the myth of consumerism influence individuals seeking careers and corporations seeking profit?

How have social and economic myths given rise to educational myths, including the myth of the average, the myth of right answers, the myth of learning units, the myth of assessment, the myth of accountability, and the myth of completion, that in turn feed the original social and economic myths?

How do different types of learning (formal learning, nonformal learning, informal learning, lifelong learning, and pervasive learning) relate to one another? How does an increasingly connected world support connectivism as a new way of learning? What economic and social impacts will result from increased connectivity? How might curriculum contours replace curriculum maps?

How do concepts of time influence society's relationship with the future? How can an Expanded Now perspective create a different perception of the future? How can past experience help individuals become more attuned to weak signals of future developments?

How can tools like the Futures Wheel, Futures Triangle, Integral Futures Matrix and Four Quadrant Mapping, and Causal Layered Analysis help with understanding the present and envisioning the future?

How can a futures learning ecosystem flourish within a complex adaptive system? How do flexible learning spaces, lifelong learning, futures literacy, connective individualism, and ecosystem engagement relate to one another within a futures learning ecosystem?

Developing Transformational Leadership Capacities

What is a "master capacity builder" (MCB) and how does this concept relate to the work of Siemens, Scharmer, Cowart,

Dweck, Grant, and Fleener and Barcinas?

How is a traditional leader different from a transformational one?

Why is it important for leaders to learn to use adaptive planning as they navigate complex adaptive systems?

How can asking appropriate questions lead to the co-creation of new ideas? What role does connective listening play in this process?

How does one design and use ecosystems formed by interconnected self-organizing networks that have the capacity to facilitate adaptation?

How can parallel processes be used for multiple purposes to promote change and ensure that "weak signals" are not missed?

What is "futures generative dialogue," and how can it be used as part of a parallel process designed to foster creativity and innovation?

How does the skill of identifying access points provide a means for moving from independence to interdependence?

How could moving from a system of organizational hierarchies to one of self-organizing groups and deep collaboration provide the kind of disruption that could lead to transformational change?

How do transformative cells function as part of a larger transformative ecosystem? How can changes in one cell lead to changes in others?

Why is transdisciplinary thinking and interaction important for breaking down silos and expanding connections and capacities?

How can the work of Master Capacity Builders lead to transformational learning? Why is it important to identify weak signals and emerging trends as part of futures work?

What does master capacity building look like in practice? Could the ideas and examples provided be recreated or adapted in other environments?

How can the workbook activities help individuals interested in building their skills as Master Capacity Builders?

Future Forward Learning

With brains brimming over with the questions listed above and others, it may be tempting for readers to let these ideas "marinate" while dealing with more urgent and pressing concerns. Indeed, it is not uncommon in current times to feel overwhelmed or lacking any capacity for additional efforts. This is where the Master Capacity Builder (MCB) idea of "moving in and out" can be empowering. Intentionally and fully engaging with transformational work whenever possible (without any expectation of perfection), while stepping away when needed, is one way to commit to supporting this important movement. Here are some potential action steps for the reader to consider:

- Share this book with someone who may be interested.

- Start a discussion group to dialogue about these ideas with your colleagues, neighbors, or friends.

- Join the COTF group (Communities of the Future) at https://communitiesofthefuture.org/ .

- Read *Preparing for a World that Doesn't Exist—Yet* by Rick

Smyre and Neil Richardson.

•Lead a group or class in one of the workbook activities.

•Contact one or more of the authors with feedback or ideas.

•Reflect on one concept that engaged you and make a connection with something you are doing right now. Could you apply it?

Although no one can know exactly what the future will look like, it is certain that change will happen. Will that change bring greater good or will society be more divided and less equal? The answer depends on the willingness of those alive today to devote time to make an impact for the future. Nobel Laureate Rabindranath Tagore is believed to have said it this way, "The one who plants trees, knowing that he or she will never sit in their shade, has at least started to understand the meaning of life." And Tagore also said, "Everything comes to us that belongs to us if we create the capacity to receive it."

References

Austin City Government. (nd). *Boomers collaborative: A residential retirement cooperative and small business incubator*. Author. http://www.austintexas.gov/edims/document.cfm?id=249153

Austin City Government. (nd). Boomers collaborative foundation. Author. https://www.boomerscollaborative.org .

Bain, A., & Weston, M. E. (2012). *The Learning Edge*. Amsterdam University Press.

Barton, D., & Moore, E. (2019, October 1). Student Applied Benchmarking: A Whole College Success Effort. League for Innovation in the Community College. https://www.league.org/innovation-showcase/student-applied-benchmarking-whole-college-student-success-effort

Berry, B., Byrd, A., & Wieder, A. (2013). *Teacherpreneurs: Innovative Teachers Who Lead But Don't Leave* (1st ed.). Jossey-Bass.

Bishop, P.C. & Hines, A. (2012 or 2016). *Teaching about the Future*. Palgrave Macmillan.

Bolick, C., & Hardiman, K. J. (2021). *Unshackled: Freeing America's K–12 Education System*. Hoover Institution Press.

Bramante, F. J., & Colby, R. L. (2012). *Off the Clock: Moving Education From Time to Competency* (1st ed.). Corwin.

Brown, B. (2015). *Daring greatly: How the courage to be vulnerable transforms the way we live, love, parent, and lead*. Penguin.

Burgess, S., & Houf, B. (2017). *Lead Like a PIRATE: Make School Amazing for Your Students and Staff*. Dave Burgess Consulting, Incorporated.

Carver, Tabitha. (2019). *Growth Rings blog post* October 19, 2019 https://growthringsjcc.blogspot.com/2019/10/growth-rings-careers-college-and-debt.html

Clark, J. K., Conley, B., & Raja, S. (2020). Essential, fragile, and invisible community food infrastructure: The role of urban governments in the United States. *Food Policy*, 102014.

COTF. (nd). Communities of the Future website. https://communitiesofthefuture.org/

CNN. (2021). *Merck and Johnson & Johnson vaccine: How the White House convinced two pharmaceutical giants to collaborate* (March). https://www.cnn.com/2021/03/03/politics/biden-merck-johnson--johnson-dpa/index.html

Clifton, J. (2011). *The Coming Jobs War*. Gallup Press.

Cowart, A. (2020). Presencing the theory U framework as foresight method, in R. Slaughter& A. Hines, (Eds), *The Knowledge Base of Futures Studies 2020*, pp. 98-108. Association of Professional Futurists.

Cunningham, C. A. (2014). *Systems theory for pragmatic schooling: Toward principles of democratic education*. New York: Palgrave Macmillan.

Couros, G. (2015). *The Innovator's Mindset: Empower Learning, Unleash Talent, and Lead a Culture of Creativity*. Dave Burgess Consulting, Incorporated.

Dator, J. (2017). Manoa's four generic images of the futures. *APF Compass*, July, 2-7. https://static1.squarespace.com/static/5bc578bdfb22a52798f8a038/t/5d1844fe53fad10001fb-f127/1561871656439/4.+Dator-4+Futures+Museum.pdf

Diamond, J. (2021). *'They just were not all in': How the White House convinced two pharmaceutical giants to collaborate on a vaccine.* CNN Politics (March 3, 2021). https://www.cnn.com/2021/03/03/politics/biden-merck-johnson--johnson-dpa/index.html.

DiMaggio, P. J., & Powell, W. W. (1983). The iron cage revisited: Institutional isomorphism and collective rationality in organizational fields. *American sociological review*, 147-160.

Domenech, D., Sherman, M., & Brown, J. L. (2016). *Personalizing 21st Century Education: A Framework for Student Success* (1st ed.). Jossey-Bass.

Doucet, A., Evers, J., Guerra, E., Lopez, N., Soskil, M., Timmers, K., & Schwab, K. (2018). *Teaching in the Fourth Industrial Revolution: Standing at the Precipice* (1st ed.). Routledge.

Dweck, C. (2008). *Mindset: The New Psychology of Success.* Ballantine Books, Inc.: NY.

Education Strategy Group (2020, p. 26), "A More Unified Community College" found at https://edstrategy.org/resource/a-more-unified-community-college/

Fleener, M.J. (2022). Futures Literacy for Adult Learning: Hopeful Futures in Complex Worlds. For Petra A. Robinson, Kamala V. Williams, Maja Stojanovic (Eds.), *Global Citizenship for Adult Education: Advancing Critical Literacies for Equity and Social Justice*, pp. 42-53. Routledge.

Fleener, M.J. (2021). A social inquiry analysis of post-pandemic higher education: a futures perspective. *Journal of Higher Education Theory and Practice, 21*(10). DOI: *https://doi.org/10.33423/jhetp.v21i10.4622*

Fleener, M.J. & Barcinas, S. (2020). Futurists' Relationships with the Future: A Study of Anticipatory Meaning-making. *Foresight* (Special Issue on North American Futures - October) Vol 22 (5/6), pp. 633-642. ISSN: 1463-6689. DOI 10.1108/FS-04-2020-0039.

Gladwell, M. (2002). *The Tipping Point: How Little Things Can Make a Big Difference.* Back Bay Books.

Grant, Adam (2021). *Think Again.* Viking: New York.

Groeschel, C. (2011). *WEIRD: Because Normal Isn't Working* (2/28/11 ed.). Zondervan.

Hargreaves, A., & Shirley, D. L. (2012). *The global fourth way: The quest for educational excellence.* Corwin Press.

Hornay, R. (2020). *Transformational Leadership in the Enterprise.* The Business of IT Blog. found at https://www.bmc.com/blogs/transformational-leadership/

Horst, G. (2019, April 20). *"The one who plants trees, knowing that he will never sit in their shade, has at least started to understand the meaning of life." (Rabindranath Tagore).* Grhgraph's Blog. https://grhgraph.wordpress.com/2019/04/20/the-one-who-plants-trees-knowing-that-he-will-never-sit-in-their-shade-has-at-least-started-to-understand-the-meaning-of-life-rabindranath-tagore/

Inayatullah, S. (2008). Six pillars: futures thinking for transforming. Foresight 10(1), pp. 4-21. https://doi.org/10.1108/14636680810855991.

Jain, S. (2001). The poet's challenge to schooling: Creative freedom for the human soul. *Udaipur, India: Shikshantar.*

Johnson, S. (2015). *Who moved my cheese?* Random House.

Kriz, C. J. (2008). *The Patient Will See You Now: How Advances in Science, Medicine, and Technology Will Lead to a Personalized Health Care System.* Rowman & Littlefield Publishers.

Kuhn, T. (1957). *The Copernican Revolution.* Harvard University Press

Kuhn, T. (1962). *Structure of Scientific Revolutions.* University of Chicago Press.

Lewis, C. (2016). *Too Fast to Think: How to Reclaim Your Creativity in a Hyper-connected Work Culture.* Kogan Page Publishers.

Li, Yun. (2021). GameStop, Reddit and Robinhood: a full recap of the historic retail trading mania on Wall Street. CNBC (January 20, 2021). https://www.cnbc.com/2021/01/30/gamestop-reddit-and-robinhood-a-full-recap-of-the-historic-retail-trading-mania-on-wall-street.html.

McKinsey & Company (2021) in "The future of work after COVID-19" found at The future of work after COVID-19 | McKinsey

McLeod, S., & Graber, J. (2018). *Harnessing Technology for Deeper Learning (A Quick Guide to*

References

Educational Technology Integration and Digital Learning Spaces) (Solutions for Creating the Learning Spaces Students Deserve) (Illustrated ed.). Solution Tree Press.

McLeod, S., & Shareski, D. (2018). *Different Schools for a Different World.* Amsterdam University Press.

Miller, R. (Ed.) (2018). *Transforming the future: Anticipation in the 21st century.* New York: Routledge.

MIT (2020), *The Work of the Future, Building Better Jobs in an Age of Intelligent Machines found at* 2020-Final-Report4.pdf (mit.edu)

Murray, T. C. (2019). *Personal & Authentic: Designing Learning Experiences That Impact a Lifetime.* Impress.

Nelson, R. (2010) Extending foresight: The case for and nature of Foresight 2.0. Futures 42(4), (May), pp. 282-294. https://doi.org/10.1016/j.futures.2009.11.014

Nussbaum-Beach, S., & Hall, L. R. (2012). *The Connected Educator.* Amsterdam University Press.

Oliver, W. L. (2019). *Not Your Mama's Classroom: What You Need to Know as a Parent About Your Child's Digital Education.* LifeWise Books.

Page, Scott (2017) Just having people who look different isn't enough to create a diverse team. *Linked In,* 9 Sep. 2017, https://www.linkedin.com/pulse/just-having-people-who-look-different-isnt-enough-create-scott-page?published=t

Perna, M. C. (2018). *Answering Why: Unleashing Passion, Purpose, and Performance in Younger Generations.* Greenleaf Book Group Press.

Pew Research Center (2021) found at file:///C:/Users/magda/Downloads/Unemployed%20Americans%20are%20feeling%20%20%20the%20emotional%20strain%20(1).pdf

Pinar, W. (1975). *Curriculum theorizing: The reconceptualists.* McCutchan

Pink, D. H. (2009). *Drive: The Surprising Truth About What Motivates Us.* Riverhead Books.

Richardson, N. at E*mergent Action* (https://emergentaction.com/neil-richardson-dc/)

Rose, T. (2016). *The End of Average: How to Succeed in a World That Values Sameness.* Penguin UK.

Rosenfeld, M.J., Thomas, R.J. & Hausen, S. (2019). *Disintermediating your friends: how online dating in the United States displaces other ways of meeting.* Proceedings of the National Academy of Sciences of the United States. Retrieved from: https://www.pnas.org/content/116/36/17753.short?rss=1

Saul, S. (2021). The pandemic hit the working class hard. The colleges that serve them are hurting, too. *New York Times,* 7 April, 2021, https://nyti.ms/3mfNqww

Scharmer, O. (2016). *Theory U: Leading from the Future as it Emerges.* Oakland: Berrett-Koehler Publishers, Inc.

Scharmer, O. (2018). *"The Essentials of Theory U" with Otto Scharmer* (video). https://www.youtube.com/watch?v=LihzvzTrOsQ

Shannon, C. J. (1948). "A Mathematical Theory of Communication." Reprinted with corrections from *The Bell System Technical Journal,* Vol. 27, pp. 379–423, 623–656, July, October, 1948. http://people.math.harvard.edu/~ctm/home/text/others/shannon/entropy/entropy.pdf

Sheninger, E. C. (2014). *Digital Leadership: Changing Paradigms for Changing Times* (1st ed.). Corwin.

Sheninger, E. C., & Murray, T. C. (2017). *Learning Transformed: 8 Keys to Designing Tomorrow's Schools, Today* (1st ed.). ASCD.

Siemens, G. (2005). Connectivism: A learning theory for the digital age. *International Journal of Instructional Technology and Distance Learning,* 2(1), 3-10. Retrieved from http://www.itdl.org/.

Smith, D. (2011). *TheNewRural. Com.* Van Haren Publishing.

Smyre, R., & Richardson, N. (2016). *Preparing for a world that doesn't exist-yet: Framing a second enlightenment to create communities of the future.* John Hunt Publishing.

Slaughter, R.A. (2020). Integral futures: theory, vision, practice. In R.A. Slaughter & A. Hines (Eds.), *The knowledge base of futures studies 2020,* pp. 237-257. Association of Professional Futurists.

Sosniak, L. A. (1994). *Bloom's taxonomy.* L. W. Anderson (Ed.). Chicago, IL: Univ. Chicago Press.

Statista. (nd.) *Online dating worldwide – statistics & facts.* https://www.statista.com/topics/7443/online-dating/#:~:text=Nearly%20280%20million%20online%20users,billion%20U.S.%20dollars%20by%202024.

Stirling, D. (2014). *Learning and Complex Adaptive Systems*. Learning Development Institute. (31 May 2014). http://www.learndev.org/dl/Stirling_Learning-CAS.pdf.

Strogatz, S. (2020). *Infinite powers: How calculus reveals the secrets of the universe*. Houghton Mifflin Harcourt. New York: New York.

Vollmer, J. R. (2010). *Schools Cannot Do It Alone*. Enlightenment Press.

Wake Tech. (nd). *What is a future forward college?* (website). https://www.waketech.edu/about-wake-tech/administrative-offices/effectiveness-and-innovation/future-forward/what-is

Wheatley, M. J. (1999). *Leadership and the New Science* (2nd ed.). Berrett-Koehler Publishers.

Whitehead, A.N. (1929). *Process and reality*. Cambridge University Press.

Wittgenstein, L. (1953/2009). *Philosophical investigations*. John Wiley & Sons.

Yeager, C. (1986). *Yeager: An Autobiography*. Bantam.

Zhao, Y. (2009). *Catching Up or Leading the Way: American Education in the Age of Globalization* (unknown ed.). ASCD.

Acknowledgements

We would like to acknowledge the leadership of Dr. Steve Scott, former president, Wake Technical Community College, and Drs. Larry Darlage and Alan Goben, former presidents of Tarrant County College, Northeast Campus, who supported sharing the master capacity builder transformational leadership concepts with students, faculty, and staff and promoted the integration of these principles in administration, planning, teaching, and student support services. We would also like to acknowledge the importance of the leadership of senior Wake Tech administrators Butch Grove and Bryan Ryan, in the implementation of these efforts. These leaders all worked with Rick Smyre and us as part of the Future Forward Colleges initiative which encouraged us to write about how these leadership principles can be applied in other ecosystems.

Appendices

Workbook Samples for Master Capacity Builders

The most important starting point for developing Master Capacity Builder skills is oneself. Expanding one's own capacities for specific skills equips one to recognize and coach capacity building in others. Therefore, a simple but specific progress chart provides checkpoints and benchmarks for an individual's expanding capacities through reflection and also through interaction and collaboration with others. Most people identify at some level on most of these characteristics, so the challenge is not to acquire these traits, but to expand our individual capacities to express and use them more beneficially and with an intent to expand the capacities of those with whom we interact. Note that Appendix A lists skills and also differentiates personal (internal) and interpersonal capacities.

APPENDIX A: PROGRESS CHART FOR BUILDING CAPACITIES FOR TRANSFORMATION:

Master Capacity Builder activity – Are you expanding your capacity for these qualities?

Focus Area- personal or interpersonal	Characteristics of Master Capacity Builders (scale of 1–10, 1 being "not much" and 10 being "often"). The goal is to move closer to 10 over a three-week period while practicing MCB skills.	Current Status	Growth Status Week 1	Growth Status Week 2	Growth Status Week 3
Personal (internal)	Openness to new Ideas				
	Willingness to take appropriate risks				
	Immense Patience				
	A passion for learning				
	Ability to identify future trends and weak signals				
	Know how to lay seeds for long-term transformation				
	Be an "and/both" connective thinker				
	Look for connections among disparate ideas and factors				
	Help each other succeed				

Interper-sonal	Ability to share thoughts and emotions				
	Ability to listen for value in what others say				
	Ability to ask appropriate questions				
	Maturity in thinking and acting				
	Concern for others				
	A balance of human, economic, moral, ethical, and spiritual values				

APPENDIX B: VALUES SYSTEM SELF-ASSESSMENT

DIRECTIONS. Place a + (plus sign) next to words or concepts you feel positive about. Place a − (minus sign) next to words or concepts you feel negative about. Cross out words or concepts that you feel neutral about.

ACTIVITY	FREEDOM	PRACTICAL-ITY
AFFECTION	FRIENDSHIP	PROGRESS
ALONE	FUTURE	RATIONAL-ITY
ANGER	GAMES	REASON
ATTENTIVE	GREED	RECRE-ATION
BOLD	GROWTH	REGRES-SIVE
BROTHERHOOD	HEALTH	RESPECT
CAREER	HUMANITARIAN	RIGH-TEOUSNESS
CHANGE	HUNGER	ROUTINE
COMFORT	IDENTITY	SAVINGS
COMPASSION	IGNORANCE	SCIENCE
CONSIDERATION	IMMORALITY	SECURITY
COOPERATION	IMPOSSIBLE	SELFISH-NESS
DECADENT	IMPROVEMENT	SELFLESS-NESS
DECISIVE	INDIVIDUALISM	SENSITIV-ITY
DEDICATION	INSENSITIVE	SOBRIETY
DEMOCRACY	INTELLECTUAL	SOCIAL
DEPENDABILITY	INTUITION	SPONTA-NEITY
DIGNITY	IRRATIONALITY	STRENGTH
DISCIPLINE	KNOWLEDGE	SYMPA-THETIC
DOMINATION	MECHANICAL	THOUGHT-LESSNESS
DUTY	MEDITATION	THRIFT
EFFICIENCY	MODERATION	TOGETHER
EMOTION	MODERN	TRUTH

ENJOYMENT	MORALITY	UNEMO-TIONAL
EQUALITY	MYSTICISM	UNITY
ERROR	NATURAL	UNUSUAL
FACT	OLD-FASHIONED	VICTORI-OUS
FALSEHOOD	ORDER	WORK
FAMILY	ORGANIZATION	
FASHIONABLE	PASSION	
FEELING	PERSONAL	

APPENDIX C: CHARACTERISTICS OF A MASTER CAPACITY BUILDER

- Openness to new ideas

- Willingness to take appropriate risks

- Immense patience

- A passion for learning

- Ability to share thoughts and emotions

- Listen for value in what others say

- Help each other succeed

- Look for connections among disparate ideas and factors

- Be an "AND/BOTH" connective thinker

- Ability to identify future trends and weak signals

- Know how to lay seeds for long-term transformation

- Ability to ask appropriate questions

- Maturity in thinking and acting

- A balance of human, moral, ethical, spiritual, and economic values

- Concern for others

APPENDIX D: RETHINKING THE FUTURE OF LEARNING

A Survey for Transformational Leaders [Faculty] as Master Capacity Builders

1) Which of the following do you consider key for preparing "learners" for a different kind of future (check all that apply):

a) The ability to see connections among disparate ideas and factors _____

b) Learning how to be a strategic planner _____

c) Scoring high on standardized tests _____

d) Develop the ability to identify weak signals _____

e) Focus on concrete outcomes _____

2) Mark each of the following from 1–5 with one being a high priority and five being a low priority.

a) Learn the principles of the science of networks _____

b) Learn how to apply the principles of complex adaptive systems _____

c) Create bubble diagrams to design effective social systems

_____

d) Build a broad and deep level of knowledge in multiple areas

_____

e) Become a connected listener _____

3) Rank order the following from 1–5 with one of high value and five of low value:

a) Become an entrepreneur _____

b) Focus on STEM skills _____

c) Learn how to ask an appropriate question _____

d) Learn how to design parallel processes _____

e) Learn the difference between reforming and transforming change _____

4) Mark each of the following from 1–5 with one being a high priority and five being a low priority.

a) Become an "and/both" thinker _____

b) Learn to think about emerging issues within a "futures con-text." _____

c) Make sure people are held accountable for outcomes when designing a transformational process _____

d) Understand how to look for "access points" _____

e) Focus on rationality, existing knowledge and measurable skills _____

5) Rank order the following from 1-5 with one being of high value and five being of low value:

a) Develop the capacities of intuition, insight, imagination and innovation _____

b) Learn how to design apps _____

c) Develop a career in one of the radical technologies _____

d) Develop a career as a coach and accelerated connector. _____

e) Learn how to identify newly emerging careers _____

6) Which of the following do you consider key to be able to insure a successful professional life in the future (check all that apply):

a) Develop the capacity to be resilient _____

b) Become flexible and adaptable _____

c) Connect with other people anywhere _____

d) Be open to new ideas _____

e) Combine great patience with the ability to take appropriate risk _____

APPENDIX E: INDENTIFYING AND ANALYZING FUTURE TRENDS AND WEAK SIGNALS

Weak signals are emerging new ideas, inventions, innovations, and discoveries that are not yet trends, but have the potential to make an impact on society (Smyre and Richardson, 2016, p. 215-16). That impact might come as disruption, augmentation, or transformation of an existing product, process, or societal pattern. Notice how this skill challenges and expands the "Open to New Ideas" characteristic of a Master Capacity Builder (see pg. 61).

Developing Capacities to Identify Weak Signals:

1) Build broad and deep knowledge in multiple areas of society.

2) Read articles and websites for those associated with cutting edge discoveries and new ideas and innovations.

3) Does the new idea or discovery cause you to think differently? If so,why?

4) Look for indirect and oblique connections to present innovative ways of doing things.

5) Would the new idea (weak signal) modify what already exists or transform the undergirding thinking in the traditional reality?

6) What are the implications if the new idea were to become the norm?

Examples:

- A loss of taste/smell was a weak signal of coronavirus infection in individuals, but it took some time before this was recognized by the medical establishment.

- The digital revolution, including the internet, was perceived as starting in the 1980s. Yet the weak signal that the revolution was on the way can be found in a 1948 article by mathematician Claude Shannon, "A Mathematical Way of Communication." (http://people.math.harvard.edu/~ctm/home/text/others/shannon/entropy/entropy.pdf) What current mathematical publication predicts our future lifestyles?

Exercise: Ask group members to spend 5 minutes searching the internet for surprising or unusual information (about anything) and making a list of the items they find. A theme is not necessary or advisable; weak signals arrive unexpectedly and have unanticipated and unpredictable impacts. Then ask participants to break into small groups, share lists, and identify connections or themes. Ask them to imagine how these micro-trends might develop, expand, or evolve as they connect or disrupt the status quo, developing a projected arc of influence/disruption. How will that weak signal impact the current situation?

APPENDIX F: PRACTICING MOVING IN AND OUT IN AN INTERPERSONAL COMMUNICATION CLASSROOM OR OTHER SMALL GROUPS.[1]

MCB Skill Focus: Moving In and Out

"Moving in and out" is the ability to adapt individual work styles and processes to those of other individuals in order to work effectively as a group to accomplish tasks.

Related MCB skills:

- Connective Thinking

- Reflecting and Connecting

Activity: Individual and Group Project
Outcomes

- Identify and analyze how verbal, nonverbal and listening behaviors impact the effectiveness of interpersonal communication within the transactional model

- Examine and evaluate how perception and self-disclosure affect the ways in which we interact with others

- Evaluate the impact of diversity using cultural dimensions in interpersonal relationships

- Analyze personal communication behaviors, including communication apprehension and emotion, and develop a skill set to become a competent communicator

- Demonstrate the use of effective assertive communication in personal and professional contexts

---

1   This activity is adapted from Wake Tech's Student Applied Benchmarking process and is used by permission.

Overview of Activity

This activity has two parts: The Individual Portion (Project description and post-Reflection) and the Group Portion (Action Proposal). Each member of the group will complete an individual activity, then the group will work together to present a proposal for action with a particular focus. The group activity will represent a cohesive proposal for transformative change that incorporates each individual project. After the group project is completed, each participant will complete and submit a reflection paper.

Guidelines

Part 1: Individual Project Report

1. Identify one aspect of your community that could be improved. This could be any aspect, including policies and procedures, communication, facilities, programs, etc. Examples from college projects include adding healthy vending machines to all campuses, starting a campus recycling program, and creating a YouTube show to provide updates on community or campus events. Ask your facilitator for ideas if you need help identifying an area for improvement.

2. Reach out to an expert in the area that you have identified to research your idea. For example, the participant who researched healthy vending machines on a college campus contacted a representative from a healthy vending machine company, while the participant who researched a recycling program contacted an expert in recycling program grants. Ask for help in identifying an expert if you have difficulty deciding who to contact. Practice effective interpersonal skills when you contact

the expert for advice and information. It is also a good idea to consult articles, books, or other sources of information to supplement the information provided by the expert.

3. After you complete your research, create a proposal for change. Include action steps and a plan for implementation.

4. Finally, present your proposal using a poster template.

Part 2: Group Portion Guidelines

Consider whether there is a common thread uniting all of your projects. Could you use this as the theme for your proposal? As a group, decide on the best way to merge your ideas into one cohesive proposal. If you have a difficult time figuring out how to incorporate elements from each person's individual project, ask your facilitator for help.

Your proposal for change can be in any format that allows you to effectively deliver your message. For example, you might use a video, a PowerPoint, a brochure, a poster, or some other format. *Each group will present one Proposal for Change to all groups.*

It is likely that deciding on a format for the presentation and sharing the work to create the proposal will be the most challenging part of this activity. Remember to use all of the Master Capacity builder skills—particularly the interpersonal collaboration skills—that you have developed to effectively co-create with your group members.

Part 3: Group Project Reflection

Write a detailed reflection of how you were able to utilize the interpersonal communication skills you developed in this exercise to successfully complete the group project.

APPENDIX G: ADAPTIVE PLANNING WORK-SHEET (Throwing the DICE)

(Adaptable for professional development, classrooms, small group planning activities, individual decisions)

Throwing the DICE: Preparing for a World that Doesn't Exist

Strategic Planning assumes that

a. one can *predict* specific outcomes, and that

b. one can *control* the processes from the starting point to the point of final destination based on experience and existing knowledge.

We all may be familiar with the SWOT analysis – Strengths, Weaknesses, Opportunities, Threats—used in strategic planning sessions. However, this type of analysis does not address the factors involved in the future-looking process of adaptive planning.

Adaptive Planning assumes that one *cannot* predict what is emerging or control all processes or potential impacts. In this case, planners need to develop processes and interlocking networks to build "capacities for transformation" that provide the ability to adapt quickly so that any individual can respond in real time to whatever appears on the horizon. In adaptive planning for community college teaching and learning, we will throw the DICE:

D – Design
I – Identify
C – Connect
E – Emerge

Design: What do we need to transform the learning experience within a futures context that includes some or all of the futures learning concepts? What would a "design" of a potential set of parallel processes look like?

Identify: Who/what are key players, factors and ideas that should be considered?

Connect: How do we go about connecting those identified in a real-time framework? What are we doing right now, and how can we evolve and expand this network to create a radical design?

Emerge: Let's imagine what might emerge with multiple platforms of learning, interlocking networks of interested people and organizations, futures projects large and small . . .

What could we design for collaborative classrooms, organizations, communities?

APPENDIX H: MCB SKILL FOCUS: CONNECTIVE THINKING

Connective thinking is the ability to see connections among disparate ideas, discoveries, processes, and people.

Related MCB skills:

• Active Listening

• Reflecting and Connecting

Activity: Paired Listening Exercise

Outcomes

• Identify and evaluate personal communication behaviors and self-awareness

• Construct steps to improve communication competence

• Describe how meaning is communicated nonverbally

• Describe the nature of listening and the challenges that can impede effective listening

• Effectively use a variety of reflective and directive listening responses

Overview of Activity

This activity will provide you with an opportunity to develop your ability to listen and ask appropriate questions in order to recognize emerging connections/patterns.

Activity Details

1. Set up a time to talk with your partner face-to-face for at least twenty minutes without interruption. Ask your partner to be prepared to describe a current problem or challenge that they are facing.

2. Meet with your partner and ask your partner to discuss the challenge. As you listen, think about how you might connect what your partner shares with something you've heard, read, or experienced that may be helpful in some way. Ask questions to broaden your understanding of the situation and your partner's reaction to this challenge.

3. After listening carefully, thank your partner for sharing. Then tell your partner at least three ways that you were able to make connections with what your partner shared. Provide at least one possible solution or next step that might be helpful to your partner.

4. Next, ask your partner to answer three questions:

   • What was helpful about how you listened?

   • What was helpful about what you shared?

   • What could you improve about your listening behaviors?

Finally, work with your partner to co-create a list of the learning that has developed as a result of the conversation. This list may include thoughts about the challenge you discussed and/or it may consist of what you learned together about listening and connecting.

If time allows, switch roles and complete steps 1-5 with the listener serving as the speaker.

Index

#MeToo 145
21st Century 7, 8, 10, 13, 20, 21, 22, 24, 26- 29, 34, 38, 42-44, 46, 67, 121, 151, 162, 163

Access points 36, 109, 121, 124, 138-139, 158, 176
Adaptive Futures Cone 73-75
Artificial intelligence 46-47, 103, 146, 149

Barcinas,Susan 115, 118, 158, 162
Barton, Denise 126, 161
Bishop, Peter 79, 161
bitcoin 145, 148
Black Lives Matter 46, 73
Black Swans 87
Blockchain 26, 98
Brown, Brene 9, 161

Capacities for transformation 1, 5, 15, 19, 35, 64, 116, 122, 127, 134, 169-170, 185, 205, 206
Carver, Tabitha 41, 161
Causal Layered Analysis (see also CLA) 88-91, 157
Center for Communities of the Future 206

Change 9, 46, 58
- adaptive 119, 123
- First Order vs. Second Order 13
- climate 6, 143, 146, 154
- deep 93, 99, 152
- educational 22, 34
- historical 17
- radical 3, 6, 118
- rapid or rate of 2, 5, 7, 13, 36, 43-44, 47, 74, 92, 102, 122, 153
- systems/societal/STEEPA 3, 5, 44, 48, 81, 126, 153,
- transformative/transformational 5-7, 9-11, 13-18, 38-39, 43, 64, 73, 85, 89, 113, 116, 122, 136, 139, 151, 155, 176, 182
- technological 77-78
Chaos and complexity 107, 118, 204
Characteristics of a Master Capacity Builder 173-174
Chruchill, Winston 147
Civilization 3-4, 11, 33-35, 69, 109
Clark, Jill K. 151, 161
Collaboration 1, 5, 23, 27, 31, 36, 54, 63, 109-111, 113, 119, 136, 147-148, 154, 158, 167
- deep 124-129, 139
Communities of the Future 1-2, 5, 6, 22, 29, 35, 40, 108, 111, 115, 159, 161, 163, 205-207
Community
- transformation 1, 29, 64, 109-110, 116, 122, 140, 205-206
Complex adaptive system 93, 118, 134, 139-140, 154, 158, 163, 175
Conley, Brian 151, 161
Connected Individuality (See connective individualism) 67, 86, 98, 117
Connection points 15, 192
Connective Individualism 5, 101, 102-103, 157
Connective learner 99

Connective listening 120-123, 130, 136-137, 139
Connectivism 15, 21, 38, 61, 87, 112-113, 120, 141, 157, 163
Consensus 17, 32-34
Consumerism 3, 11-12, 54, 58, 86, 156
Continuous innovation (see also Innovation) 121, 128, 206,
Couros, George 9, 161
COVID
  - learning in an age of 11-15, 26, 95
  - community impact 36, 46-47, 63, 80-82, 125, 150, 154, 162
Cowart, Adam 114, 157, 161
Creative Connections 15, 136-138
Creativity 12, 23, 25, 41, 57, 61, 87, 100, 102-103, 109, 112,
126, 133, 135-137, 151, 158, 161, 162
Critical thinking (see also futures critical thinking) 101, 112,
121, 147, 151
Cunningham, Craig 70, 161
Curriculum 5, 25-26, 53, 56-57, 64-65, 77, 95, 97, 107, 110,
145, 157
  - adaptive 25

Dator, James 84, 161, 162
Deepening the future 88
Democracy 2-4, 16, 33, 171
Dewey, John 71, 97
DiMaggio, Paul J. 119, 162
Diversity 6, 56, 102, 107, 117, 122, 128, 140, 147, 181
Dweck, Carol 115, 158, 162

Ecosystem (learning, see learning ecosystem)
Education
  - formal, informal, nonformal 4, 5, 9, 29, 51, 53, 54, 59, 62,
97, 98, 100-101, 103
Emergence, emergent 4, 9, 16-19, 22, 24, 27, 31, 33, 34, 36, 42,
54, 58, 62, 64, 76, 79, 80, 87, 98-100, 107, 117, 115, 119, 126,

131, 134, 147, 163, 206
Enlightenment 11, 53, 155, 163, 164,
Expanded Now 70-78, 85, 99, 114, 157

Fleener, M Jayne 114, 115, 118, 158, 162
Flexible learning spaces 5, 94, 96, 103, 157
Formal education 4, 5, 9, 29, 51, 53, 54, 59, 62, 97, 98, 100, 101, 103
Formal learning (see Learning, formal)
Future forward l(College learning) 111, 127, 154, 159, 164, 165
Futures
    - cone 70, 73-75, 83, 114
    - context 19, 23, 25-26, 79, 96, 107, 109, 111, 116, 121-124, 128-129, 141, 176, 186
    - generative dialogue 18, 31-37, 102, 119-120, 123, 135, 142, 158, 206
    - learning (see also Futures literacy) 2, 5, 6, 51, 66, 74, 75, 93-95, 97, 99, 100-105, 110, 112, 133, 157, 186
    - literate (see also Futures learning) 5, 100, 101, 103, 114, 130, 157, 162
    - matrix 82, 84, 157
    - possible, plausible and desirable 6, 44, 70, 73, 84
    - triangle 83-84, 157
    - wheel 79-82, 88, 157

Gamestop 127, 148, 162
Global Connections Television 111
Grant, Adam 115, 158, 162

Hargreaves, Andy 9, 162
Healthcare 2, 95, 126, 130, 146, 206
Higher education 119, 127, 151, 162
Hines, Andy 79, 161
Holistic thinking 20, 25, 41, 44, 95, 109, 121, 153

Hornay, Rachel 108, 162

Imagination 12, 23, 25, 100, 134, 176
Inayatullah, Sohail 75, 88, 162
Industrial Age 1, 13, 35, 205, 206
Innovation 68, 100, 101, 111, 121, 123, 126-129, 133-135, 151, 158, 161, 164, 176, 179, 206
Integral Futures 82, 84, 88, 157, 163
Interconnected 1, 5-6, 24, 29, 34, 36-37, 44, 60, 80, 99, 102, 104, 120, 158, 205
Interdependent 6, 28, 40, 44, 47, 99, 117, 124, 137
Interlocking networks 35, 119-120, 122, 124, 134-135, 137, 140, 185, 186
Intuition 19, 99-100, 134, 171, 176

Jobs, Steven 77
Johnson, Spencer 36, 162

Kauffmann Foundation 126
Kuhn, Thomas 3, 162

Latinx 146, 150
Leadership (see also Master Capacity Building) 1, 4, 5, 27, 56, 97, 105, 107-113, 115-119, 130, 133-134, 136, 140-141, 145-147, 149, 151-152, 154, 157, 162, 163, 164, 165, 205
Leadership principles 109, 115-130, 149, 154
Learning
  - contours 64, 94
  - ecosystem 4, 6, 11, 24-26, 48, 92, 93-95, 101-104, 107, 110, 157
  - ecosystem design essentials 24-26
  - heart and gut 71-72, 99
  - lifelong 5, 26, 60-61, 98-100, 103, 157
  - pervasive 5, 6, 55, 59-62, 64, 66, 97, 100, 113, 157
  - terrain (see also learning contours) 5, 65-66
Learning Community 26-27, 118
Learning systems 29, 93

Lewis, Chris 9, 162

Lifelong Learning (see learning - lifelong)

Master Capacity Builder
  - strategies 144

Master Capacity Builder 1, 105, 107-120, 130, 133, 138-144, 145, 148-150, 153-154, 157, 159, 165, 167, 169, 173, 175, 179, 183, 205

Master Capacity Builder's Toolkit 130

Master Capacity Building

McKinsey & Company 150, 162

Mental Models 14, 16, 17, 22, 31-32, 43,

Metaphors 2, 5, 44, 51, 53, 86, 89, 91, 101

Metaphor
  - third rail 48-51, 156
  - student-as-navigator 97

Miller, Riel 74, 163

Miller, William 111

Mindflex 25, 42, 101, 115

Modern Era 3, 46, 54-56, 85-88, 103-104

Monroe Community College 153

Moore, Emily 126, 161

Myths
  - educational 5, 55-59
  - learning 51-54, 62, 87
  - social/economic 52-54, 59, 86

Myths 4, 51, 67, 76, 85-86, 88-91, 98, 101, 157

National Clearninghouse Research Center 151

New Normal 13, 36, 43, 81

New York Times 151, 163

Non-linear capacity building (see also Master Capacity Builder) 137-138

Parallel Processes 15, 18, 20, 22, 24, 39, 96, 99, 122-123, 130, 134, 136-138, 140-141, 145, 148, 158, 176, 186, 206

Perna, Mark 9, 163

Pew Research Center 150, 163

pH Ecosystem 126, 206

Pinar, William 110
Powell, Walter W. 119, 162
Prince George Community College 153

Raja, Samina 151, 161
Reddit 127, 148, 162
Reflection (for master capacity building) 141, 154, 167, 182
Richardson, Neil 9-10, 67, 102, 108, 109, 115-116, 123-124, 126, 128, 134, 138, 147, 160, 163, 179
Risk
  - taking 12, 16, 35, 36, 43, 46, 56-57, 74, 114, 136, 153, 169, 173, 177
Robin-Hood 127, 148, 162
Rosenfeld, Michael 20, 163
Rumsfield, Donald 83

Scharmer, Otto 113, 157, 163
Scott, Stephen 126, 165
Seeding new ideas 46, 65, 76, 100 122, 134, 137, 139, 142, 169, 173
Seeds of Doubt 50-51
Seeing with soft eyes 73, 99-100,
Seeing-as differently 73-74, 99
Seimens, George 15
Self-organization 117, 125, 130-131, 206
Self-organize (see also Self-organization) 119, 126, 127
Shirley, Dennis 9, 162
Slaughter, Richard 161, 163,
Smyre, Rick iii, v, 1, 9, 10, 67, 102, 107, 108, 109, 111, 115, 116, 123, 124, 126, 128, 134, 138, 139, 147, 160, 163, 165, 179, 202, 203
Statista 21, 163
STEEPA 3, 5, 80-82
Stirling, Diana 118, 163
Strogatz, Steven 118, 164

Tagore, Rabindranath 160, 162
Teaching and learning 7, 8, 24, 28, 37, 111, 156, 185

Telemetry 26
Theory U 112-113, 161, 163
Transdisciplinary thinking 128, 130, 158
Transformation
  - community 1, 29, 64, 109, 110, 116, 122, 140, 205, 206
Transformational
  - challenges 67-69, 88
  - leadership 4, 27, 105, 107-110, 115-118, 133, 136, 145, 149, 152, 154, 157, 162, 165, 203
  - learning 4, 15, 20, 26, 44, 95, 107-108, 110, 126, 128, 130, 133, 144, 147, 159, 206
Transformative Cells (see also transformative ecosystems) 126-127, 158
Transformative Change 6, 10, 38, 64, 73, 109, 116, 139, 151, 182
Transitional times 6, 51, 86
Trends 7, 38, 61, 122, 123, 128, 129, 134-135, 140, 142, 145, 159, 169, 173, 179, 180

UNESCO 101
Unlearning 15-16, 99, 115, 142-143, 154
Uplearning 15, 17, 26, 99, 115, 142-143, 154
Upskilling 149-150, 154

Wake Tech Future Forward College 111, 164, 165
Wake Technical Community College 125, 165
Weak signals 38, 78, 81, 119, 123, 128-130, 134, 140, 142, 154, 157-159, 169, 173, 175, 179-180
Whitehead, Alfred North 70, 164
Wilber, Ken 84
Wittgenstein, Ludwig 73, 85, 164

Yeager, Chuck 16-17, 38, 164

About the Authors

Professional Backgrounds

Benita Budd, Professor and Future Forward Fellow at Wake Technical Community College, Raleigh, North Carolina ba-budd@gmail.com

John Carver, Educational Consultant, Blogger, Thought Leader, Senior Planning and Research Associate for the Center for Educational Leadership and Technology (CELT), former classroom teacher, activities director, secondary principal, and Superintendent of Schools (Iowa and Tennessee). Jccarver56@gmail.com

Dr. Magdalena H. de la Teja, Retired Vice President from Tarrant County College; Consultant, Coach and Mentor residing in Austin, Texas. magdalena.delateja@gmail.com. https://www.linkedin.com/in/magdalena-h-de-la-teja-a532b73a/

Dr. M. Jayne Fleener, Professor and former dean, colleges of education at Louisiana State University and North Carolina State University; jfleener4@gmail.com; Personal Website: https://blockchaineducation.info/; LinkedIn: https://www.

linkedin.com/in/jaynefleener/; Twitter: @mjaynefleener

Emily Moore, Associate Professor and Department Head, Communications, Wake Technical Community College, Raleigh, North Carolina. ecmoore@waketech.edu

Personal Biographies

Benita Budd, Professor and Future Forward Fellow at Wake Technical Community College, Raleigh, North Carolina, developed a long-term benchmark project with Rick Smyre to promote and implement Master Capacity Building and other futures-oriented concepts as Wake Tech became identified as the founding Future Forward College within the Communities of the Future framework. She conceptualized and organized a series of Future Forward Summits at Wake Tech and continues to introduce concepts and collaborative processes through workshops and conferences. Her collaboration with college students, faculty, and administrators, as well as leaders in community development and public policy is an ever-transforming work in progress to explore, adapt, and discover new capacities for transformation.

John C. Carver, lifelong educator and digital innovator for public schools and communities, discusses the factors that propel the urgency for transformational change, including technological advances, economic disruptions, and social pressures that put our 19th and 20th century institutions in need of metamorphosis. He has worked with Rick Smyre and Communities of the Future in developing futures-oriented concepts for several decades. As an early Master Capacity Builder, he led school districts in Iowa and Tennessee into the digital age, and his insights expanded the capacities of school districts and communities to work together for the betterment of all. He envisions the learning ecosystems of the future that is the Second Enlightenment, and he provides a checklist of requirements for a viable, sustainable transformation.

Dr. Magdalena H. de la Teja, Vice President, Tarrant County College in Ft. Worth, Texas (ret.); Consultant, Coach and Mentor residing in Austin, Texas.

Dr. de la Teja brings the critically important perspective of student and community issues to the discussion of transformative learning. Her work with Rick Smyre at Tarrant County College dates from 2012 and has led to long-term collaborations with members of the Wake Tech academic community. She addresses the urgent need to recognize and respond to the realities of underserved, often minoritized communities, including the effects of poverty and inequitable opportunities to access education and employment. Inequities and inadequacies of traditional systems are worse than ineffective; they are restrictive and often oppressive. Her travels in all continents of the world have enriched her understandings of our diverse humanity and nature's vulnerabilities which impact our own. Change that is transformative comes through Master Capacity Builder (MCB) transformational leadership. MCB leaders utilize connective behaviors that build diverse networks and ecosystems. And through collaboration and personal capacities what results is a reorientation/broadening of perspectives as refreshing alternatives to rearranging old ideas and methods. https://www.linkedin.com/in/magdalena-h-de-la-teja-a532b73a/

Dr. M. Jayne Fleener, Professor, former dean, Louisiana State University and North Carolina State University, residing in Raleigh, NC.

Dr. Fleener has been a part of the Communities of the Future since approximately 2014. Her work has included participating in COTF 2.0 discussions to support the transformation of the COTF initiative as it moves forward, and working with colleagues at Wake Tech in their Futures Forward initiative. Her publications span over 30 years, focusing on transformational change in education and society. Her two previous books, *Curriculum Dynamics: Recreating Heart* and *Chaos, Complexity, Curriculum and Culture: A Conversation* (edited) explore postmodern logics and emergent systems change.

Emily Moore, Department Head, Communication and Theatre at Wake Technical Community College, brings insights for expanding capacities in diverse groups through Reflective practices and Connectivism, pushing the boundaries of the classroom and collaboration. Her experiences as a kindergarten teacher, parent involvement coordinator in public schools, and communications professor and administrator have enriched her Master Capacity Builder skills when working with diverse groups-- by age, culture, race, or roles in the system. Her projects and publications –involving student benchmarking, civility projects, reflective practices, and teaching with emotional intelligence -- demonstrate the effectiveness of these approaches that remove the limiting silos of academic hierarchies, subject matter, and conventional pedagogy. Like all busy professionals, Emily believes that moving in and out of innovative work allows people to live a healthier and more balanced life.

About Communities of the Future

In 1989, a group of twelve people from North and South Carolina met at Wilmington, NC to ask the question, "how do we get people in the Southeast interested in thinking about the future." From the dialogue of that weekend was birthed the idea of Communities of the Future (COTF). Over the next twenty-six years, a network of people in forty-seven states in the US and eleven other countries of the world has evolved, working in collaboration to develop new concepts, methods and techniques of community transformation. A virtual COTF Center was established in 1993 using the Internet to network those involved. The COTF Network continually "morphs" by adding "nodes" through collaboration with existing people and organizations throughout the country when new COTF concepts and methods are created.

Based on the idea that we are living in a time of historical transformation, the Communities of the Future Network has focused on a new concept of leadership called Master Capacity Builders to develop new "capacities for transformation" capable of helping local areas prepare for a constantly changing, interconnected and increasingly complex society. Over the last decade, it has become apparent that many principles, concepts and methods of an Industrial Age society have become increasingly obsolete. Communities of the Future is an experiment in community research and development to identify and develop new approaches to how we do economic development, how we govern, how we educate/learn, how we create a community-based system of preventive healthcare, how we lead, and especially how we think.

New ideas have begun to emerge which will be necessary to sustain a dynamic society. Concepts such as Transformational Learning, Mobile Collaborative Governance & Creative Molecular Economy, and pH Ecosystem for preventive healthcare are emerging which challenge the very undergirding principles of Industrial Age institutions. Although standards will still be important in key areas of life such as manufacturing and evaluation of best practices, the very nature of transformational change demands the ability to establish flexible rules and alternative ways of thinking. People and organizations will need to learn how to adapt to the uncertainty and ambiguity of an emerging society based on principles of self-organization, interdependency and continuous innovation.

The Center for Communities of the Future emphasizes "futures generative dialogue" of "early adapters" (people who are open to new ideas). Once new ideas are identified through the facilitation of small networks of creative thinkers, local "futures projects" are established to introduce one or more new "capacities for transformation" into the thinking and activities of local communities to see what resonates and what is inappropriate. COTF is pioneering new concepts, methods and techniques of community transformation to be used in parallel to other basic strategic planning models. The goal is to spread "capacities for transformation" throughout any organization/community in a dynamic and flexible way. It is in this way that the concepts and methods of COTF reflect the use of ecological principles of self-organization, continuous innovation and emergence. The COTF web site at www.communitiesofthefuture.org provides a central learning location for one to be introduced to COTF concepts and methods.

Printed in the USA
CPSIA information can be obtained
at www.ICGtesting.com
LVHW081746031123
762986LV00046B/1053